Women Travellers in the Near East

Women Travellers in the Near East

edited by

Sarah Searight

ASTENE and Oxbow Books

Published by
Oxbow Books, Park End Place, Oxford OX1 1HN

© Oxbow Books and the individual authors, 2005

ISBN 1-84217-161-5

A CIP record for this book is available from the British Library

This book is available from

Oxbow Books, Park End Place, Oxford OX1 1HN
(Phone: 01865-241249; Fax: 01865-794449)

and

The David Brown Book Co.
PO Box 511, Oakville, CT 06779
Tel: (860) 945–9329; Fax: (860) 945–9468

or from our website
www.oxbowbooks.com

Cover image: Members of the Single Lady Missionaries of the United Presbyterian Mission of North America, c.1892/1893. Published courtesy of the Presbyterian Historical Society, Presbyterian Church U.S.A. (Philadelphia, PA).

Printed in Great Britain by
Antony Rowe, Chippenham

Contents

Illustrations

Contributors

Dorothy Anderson has worked for an international library organisation and was director of a programme developing national bibliographies and bibliographic standards. Publications include *Miss Irby and her Friends*, *The Balkan Volunteers* and *Baker Pasha: misconduct and mischance*; she has also written several contributions to the *Oxford Dictionary of National Biography*. She is currently at work on another Victorian biography.

Elizabeth French is the daughter of archaeologists and herself studied archaeology at Cambridge and the Institute of Archaeology, University of London in the 1950s. She was wife to the Director of the British Institute of Archaeology at Ankara and herself Director of the British School at Athens.

Deborah Manley is a founder member of the Association for the Study of Travel in Egypt and the Near East. She wrote with her sister, Peta Rée, the biography of Henry Salt, consul-general in Egypt 1816–27 (2001), and with Dr Sahar Abdel Hakim, *Travelling through Egypt* (2004), a collection of the accounts of travellers in Egypt through two millennia.

Charles Plouviez (MA Edinburgh) spent 34 years in advertising and since retiring has written and published articles on various literary and other subjects, including three contributions to the *Oxford Dictionary of National Biography*.

Megan Price is currently researching for a D.Phil at Oxford University on *Town and Gown, Amateur and Professional Archaeology in Oxford 1850–1900*. In this, she is tracing the contributions made by 'neglected amateurs' to today's discipline of British prehistoric archaeology. She has already a BA and Master of Studies in Archaeology. She was previously a head teacher.

Sarah Searight (MA Oxon, MA London, Islamic Art & Architecture) has travelled and worked all over the Middle East. Publications include *The British in the Middle East, Steaming East, Yemen: Land and People*. She was a founding member of ASTENE and its first honorary secretary and currently chairs the Society for Arabian Studies.

Janet Starkey studied Anthropology at Edinburgh University and then at SOAS, University of London and currently lectures in the 'Anthropology of the Middle East' and on 'The Mediterranean Basin Region' at the University of Durham. She has worked in the Gulf, Jordan, Egypt and the Sudan, as well as in the Department of Ethnography, British Museum. She has written or edited several books on travellers in the Middle East as well as on the Beja of the Eastern Desert of Egypt and the Sudan. She is currently working on Alexander Russell, MD, a Scottish doctor in eighteenth century Aleppo.

Alix Wilkinson (PhD in Linguistics, Georgetown University; Fellow in Landscape Studies at Dumbarton Oaks, Harvard) is the author of *The Garden in Ancient Egypt* (London, Rubicon Press, 1998) and *Ancient Egyptian Jewellery* (London, Methuen 1972). She is the honorary secretary of the Association for the Study of Travel in Egypt and the Near East and a member of the Garden History Society and of London Historic Parks and Gardens Trust.

Jeanne Marie Warzeski wrote her doctoral thesis on 'US Women in Egypt 1854–1914'. She has worked extensively in museum curatorial and cultural resources fields and she is currently Chief of History, Collections & Cultural Resources, Pamplin Historical Park & National Resources Museum of the Civil War Soldier, Petersburg, Virgina, USA.

1. Introduction

Sarah Searight

It is a privilege to edit a volume of travels about such stalwart members of my sex. Modern feminism has often brought them to the fore although they were quite prominent in their day too. They were educated, enlightened, sometimes romantic, several had private incomes that facilitated their roaming, as a rule not much concerned with public opinion back home which was sometimes wary of their independence. Unlike some of the male travellers they were essentially 'amateurs' and travelled as independents. They were physically and mentally resilient, above all they were inquisitive, though occasionally not as much as one would like; curiosity is an essential characteristic in a traveller, not always the case with today's globe trotter, arguably more often found in the female sex than in the male, reaching out to the exotic. Several could wield articulate pens; this was crucial; it helped pay for the travel and it enables us to enjoy them today. In several cases exotic travel granted precious anonymity. They are sometimes rather tiresome in their eccentricities and most were, by the very fact of their travels, eccentrics.

Some travelled alone, a few with companions. Most were transient; only the doughty Miss Irby, Lucie Duff Gordon, Emmeline Lott and the American missionaries actually settled down. None of them was particularly 'adventurous', nor indeed exposed to particular hardship with the exception of the loyal Sarah Belzoni traipsing after her husband and the undaunted Isabella Bird in the Sinai peninsula. The horizons of their travels were limited, with the exception of Miss Muir Mackenzie and Miss Irby in the Balkans and perhaps Isabella Bird in Sinai. On the whole the horizons were the Classical world for those in the eastern Mediterranean or the blessed Nile; even Lucie hardly left its banks. For most of them the main hazards of their travel were plague and cholera; here the exceptions are the valiant Misses Muir Mackenzie and Irby in the maelstrom of Balkan upheavals. Some were changed by the experience of travel; that comes across even in the conventional literary form of 'letters' that several adopted.

'Don't tell anyone that the me they knew will not come back in the me that returns,' wrote Gertrude Bell in one of hers, not included here but it might have been an appropriate warning for those who are included.[1]

Being women gave them potentially a breadth of vision denied to men; physically they could see both sides of the harim, mentally a wider perspective. None, however, had the unique advantage of Jan Morris: 'I have had the peculiar experience of travelling both as a man and as a woman, and I have reached the conclusion, on the whole, that during my own travelling years the female traveller has had it easier than the male. To this day the human sorority is stronger by far than the fraternity.'[2]

The world in which they travelled was that of the Ottoman Empire, including what we now refer to as the Balkans, Egypt and the Near East of Turkey, Syria, Lebanon and Palestine/Israel. The late eighteenth and nineteenth centuries were a time of cultural as well as economic upheaval. After 1789 Europe was in a post-Revolution ferment that led willy nilly to all sorts of changes in outlook not least in the slow social emancipation of women; moreover the Ottoman Empire was only gradually recovering from the trauma of Napoleon's invasion and occupation of Egypt in 1798. The Near East of the Ottoman Empire was already in the thrall of European commercial links at the time of the invasion but the effects of that invasion, the violent exposure of Ottoman weakness, were to last throughout the nineteenth century leading ultimately, a hundred and twenty years later, to the demise of the Empire itself.

The economic involvement of Europeans in the Ottoman Empire had been developing slowly since the Ottoman capture of Constantinople in 1453. It grew considerably in the sixteenth century, especially during the reign of Suleyman the Magnificent, and by the end of that century French and then English merchants had joined longstanding Venetian and Genoese trading communities to take advantage of Ottoman patronage for European goods, even more for access to oriental commodities – textiles and coffee among them. By the seventeenth century there were European merchants at such major Silk Road termini as Constantinople, Smyrna/Izmir and Aleppo, as well as Beirut and Alexandria. By the eighteenth century economic concerns were leading inevitably to political interest, hence the appointment in 1717 of Britain's first ambassador to the Ottoman Porte (the title referred to the 'Gate' that signified the office of the Grand Vizier, chief official of the Ottoman government). That ambassador was Edward Wortley Montagu, the rather insignificant husband of the much better known Lady Mary.

Along with this economic and political interest came interest in the ancient

---

[1] G. Bell, *Letters* (London, 1927).

[2] Foreword to Dea Birkett, *Off the Beaten Track: Three Centuries of Women Travellers* (London, 2004), 11.

Near East. This included the centuries-old curiosity about the extraordinary relics of Pharaonic Egypt that were gradually becoming more accessible to courageous travellers up the Nile (we shall see Lucie Duff Gordon complaining about the streams of tourists attracted to those by improving facilities in the 1860s). As travel within other parts of the Ottoman Empire became easier and safer, the interest grew to include the classical Near East, the ruins of Asia Minor as well as those of Greece and Aegean islands, Hellenistic caravan cities such as Pergamon, Ephesus, Baalbek. The steady growth of travel 'beyond the Grand Tour' developed from the Renaissance revival of classical knowledge: if you had the benefit of a classical education, a passion for antiquity and a private income you might well be inclined either to set out yourself or pay for someone else to go and bring back a few odds and ends of antique stones to decorate your patch of English landscape. There were even glimmers of interest in contemporary society, not just the Christian Holy Land but also the Muslim world surrounding the traveller. But, with the exception of Lady Mary Wortley Montagu, whose *Letters*[3] have been such a success ever since their publication in 1763, the travellers were all men.

So when the French invaded Egypt travellers had already made a considerable contribution to knowledge of the region and a flourishing literature. Napoleon's so-called army of *savants* is well known, the impact of their *Déscription de l'Égypte* perhaps exaggerated. But the ease of that French occupation, however brief, led by slow degrees to ever greater involvement of Europeans in Egyptian and also Ottoman affairs.

Now, how do our ladies at large fit into this picture? Why did they take so intrepidly to the high road to the East? Of course they were inquisitive. They were moderately spiritual – Princess Caroline heading for Jerusalem (and more generous to its Christian residents than some visitors), Isabella Bird on her pilgrimage to St Catherine's in Sinai, the American missionaries. Some were caught up in the elucidation of the ancient civilisations that are so tantalisingly visible in this part of the world – those archaeological wives. One woman, Amelia Edwards, travelled up the Nile to escape the dreadful European weather (a familiar excuse) and went on to found the Egypt Exploration Society. Some travelled for professional reasons: Henrietta Liston accompanying her ambassadorial husband, Emmeline Lott employed as governess in Egypt, the missionaries again. Only Lucie had the poignancy of her illness.

They were good improvisers – with servants and guides, with food, with the rudiments of medicine and first aid. Both Lucie and Isabella were greeted with cries of 'Hakim! Hakim! Doctor! Doctor!' by locals wherever they went, Lucie often into cholera-stricken communities. 'I have affected some brilliant cures,'

---

[3] Lady Mary Wortley Montagu, *The Travel Letters of Mary Wortley Montagu* (London, 1763).

she told her daughter Janet.[4] They had problems with their own health, Lucie the obvious example, Isabella always, the Misses Muir Mackenzie and Irby also (in fact Georgina Muir Mackenzie had to give up her educational mission in the Balkans for reasons of poor health). Some went in for local dress; Lucie worried that her husband Alexander visiting her in Cairo would be upset by her baggy pants and loose tunic but tactfully she doesn't tell us that he was. On the whole, easy-fitting ethnic garments versus stays was a matter of choice and perhaps if you have always worn stays it would be uncomfortable without.

I would like first to introduce Mrs, later Lady, Liston, who certainly kept her stays on, refusing to shed them in the bath house despite pleas from women customers. Henrietta Marchant in 1796, at the age of forty-five, married the Scottish diplomat Robert Liston who had just returned from three years as ambassador to the Ottoman Porte. They were immediately sent to Philadelphia, to the newly fledged American government. By 1812, however, having returned from the US, they were heading east, Liston having once again been appointed ambassador in Constantinople. His posting there lasted until 1820.

As Deborah Manley points out in her essay on Mrs Liston, Henrietta was an interested observer determined to describe her impressions in the manner of that previous ambassadress, Lady Mary. Like Lady Mary they are contained in letters, now in the National Library of Scotland. 1812 was not a good time to travel across Europe; instead the Listons had a horrible voyage to the Mediterranean, though slightly better thereafter. Most of Henrietta's impressions relate to her early days in the embassy, in the traditionally European quarter of Pera, in 1813; they describe the sort of curiosities expected by her reading public and which still strike a chord with a tourist today – the harim (ever popular with women, one up on their male contemporaries), the bath house (where she was much more modest than Lady Mary and refused point blank to participate: 'I was impatient to get out with all my clothes upon my back,' she wrote),[5] the dervishes, the departure of the annual Muslim pilgrimage to Mecca, an embassy ball. There was also the perennial hazard of the plague, keeping the embassy and its staff confined to quarters until it abated. They went on leave in 1815 when Liston was knighted, returned to Constantinople and finally left in 1821.

Liston's first ambassadorial posting in the Ottoman capital coincided with that of a thoroughly sophisticated French diplomat, Comte de Choiseul-Gouffier, who was responsible amongst other things for employing an artist to record the Ottoman scene. He was also the host (an excellent host, I have always imagined) of another of our ladies, the notorious ('*infinitamente* indiscreet', according to Horace Walpole commenting on her divorce and self-imposed exile)[6] Elizabeth

[4] Letter, February 7th, 1865.
[5] National Library of Scotland. S709.f.70.
[6] *DNB*, 'Anspach, Elizabeth, Margravine'.

Craven. Lady Craven as she chose to be known in 1785 (actually the Margravine of Anspach) when she set off from Paris to visit the aristocratic community around Central Europe, Russia and the Crimea before turning up in Constantinople, again uses the useful medium of letters to describe her adventures, in her case addressed most nobly to the Margrave of Brandebourg (another of her hosts). They were in due course published as *A Journey through the Crimea to Constantinople*. There she exhibits a fairly typical range of prejudices: Turkish men are lazy, fat and stupid, women are free from all reproach. She has no time for Islam and reckons mosques ideal places for intrigue because 'a figure wrapped up like a mummy can easily kneel down by another without being suspected, and mutter in a whisper any sort of thing' – shades of early anti-terrorist fears we are all too familiar with nowadays.[7]

Choiseul-Gouffier provided her with the wherewithal – the frigate *Tarleton* – to proceed to Greece. In Athens she nearly pre-empted Elgin, tempted to pick up a piece of the Parthenon but was warned by her host that the Turks were adamantly against any such action. That didn't stop her proposing to the recipient of her letters that the Austrian Emperor could collect a few fragments of the sculpture of the so-called Temple of Minerva (i.e. the Parthenon), 'to preserve them as examples to this or rising generations.'[8]

The Listons as well as the 'feisty ladies' of Charles Plouviez' essay, Lady Craven and Princess Caroline, all comment disapprovingly on removal of stones from the Acropolis, Henrietta Liston writing of 'the Patreism or Selfishism of a former British Ambassador' who had removed a caryatid (and also, it must be said, one or two other remarkable stones). But of these 'enlightened' ladies only Caroline, the somewhat maligned Princess of Wales, feels an affinity with the world in which she was travelling; was this perhaps because she was so out of kilter with her own European *monde*? Social outcasts such as Caroline, and also her contemporary Lady Hester Stanhope (who refused to meet Caroline and described her as 'a downright whore'),[9] were more at ease in an alien world; one can think of any number of modern examples of alienated 'expatriates' today.

Lucie Duff Gordon was no social outcast – far from it. But she was an exile, fighting her tuberculosis in an environment with which, through her seven years in Egypt, she felt increasingly more at ease than with family and circle back home in England. She is perhaps the most interesting commentator on that local scene – Luxor, its surroundings and its people – one small but important reason being that she learnt to speak Arabic fluently as well as read and write it enough to be able to discuss issues, problems and happiness with those around her. It is interesting to speculate why her *Letters* continue to be republished: is it for the

---

[7] Craven, *Letters* LXVV, 189.
[8] *Ibid.*, 225.
[9] Christopher Hibbert, *George III: a personal history* (London, Viking, 1998), 355.

poignancy of her fight with disease, or for her comments on the contemporary Egyptian scene? The transience of the modern tourist industry, buying the copies well distributed in Egyptian hotel bookshops, suggests the former (and arguably Lucie and/or her family editors traded on this) but many of her comments on life in Egypt are as relevant today as in the mid-nineteenth century.

An earlier sympathetic reporter was the shadowy Sarah Belzoni, English wife of the Italian strong-arm Giovanni who came to Egypt in 1816 to persuade the Viceroy to employ him on hydraulics. That was a failure but Belzoni was able to put his strong arm techniques to the removal of gigantic stones from Pharaonic sites along the Nile. He was a true bombast but it is his wife's *Trifling Account*, appended to his *Narrative* of his operations, that strikes a chord today. Sarah was the one exception to my initial paragraph: she was neither well educated nor possessed of a private income but resourceful she certainly was, left alone for instance for two months at Philae where her only visitors were local women. Her account is rather more colourful and individual than Giovanni's.

Increasingly, in the nineteenth century, women visiting the region are as absorbed in the archaeology as the men are; we see that in the essay on Amelia Edwards and Margaret Benson. Amelia founded the Egypt Exploration Society, still going strong today, and Margaret was actually able to study the new academic discipline of Egyptology at London University. The essay on the wives of archaeologists is particularly interesting in this respect, describing three such women working with their husbands on ancient Middle Eastern sites and in their accounts able to describe not only the sites in terms accessible to the general reader (often important for funding purposes) but also the local world in which they were operating.

'In which they were operating': this meant familiarity with the language and not just kitchen Arabic. This was Lucie's great asset, acknowledged in her letters but more difficult to trace in the other women included here. Two exceptions were two young ladies of independent means, Georgina Muir Mackenzie and Paulina Irby who in 1859 decided to explore parts of the Balkans. So enmeshed did they become in the troubled region, such ardent champions of the 'southern Slavs', that they learnt Serbo-Croat as well as some Bulgarian, in order to develop their own special mission: to improve the conditions of Christian Slav women through education. Theirs, like Lucie's, is a remarkable story of optimism despite all the odds; Paulina eventually died in Sarajevo in 1911.

In many ways the bravest of all was well educated but of limited means – Emmeline Lott who went to Egypt in 1862 as governess to the Khedive Ismail's son Ibrahim. One has enormous sympathy for the governesses of the Victorian era, many of them perhaps making use of the Female Middle Class Emigration Society (what a fate) though Emmeline was probably not one of them. At least she was articulate and had a certain success with her pen, describing her fairly horrendous experiences in the Khedivial establishment in several publications. Taking the train from Alexandria to Cairo in 1862 to take up her appointment, a fellow passenger, a Greek merchant, urged her most emphatically 'to abandon the idea of entering His Highness's service.' She ignored the advice, luckily for us, as she was able to give us a glimpse of the strange, almost anachronistic world inhabited by the women of the Khedivial world.

Isabella Bird described letters (most of her accounts were in that form) as 'the best mode of placing the reader in the position of the traveller, and of enabling him to share, not only first impressions in their original vividness, and the interests and enjoyment of travelling, but the hardships, difficulties and tedium which are their frequent accompaniments.' She above all should know. Travel writers today fill their accounts with strange conversations, usually in direct speech, which add little to our understanding of the world in which they are conversing and raise doubts as to whether they actually took place. Surprisingly, there is more sense of immediacy in these equally contrived 'letters' than in any number of chats on the spot. Personalities emerge; I have a sense of their being 'my' women, women in every case I would so like to have met.

All these women were looking for outlets for their energy and intelligence in this Near Eastern world; perhaps one should count them amongst the earliest career seekers. It is interesting in this context to look at the American women missionaries who came to Egypt at the end of the nineteenth century, seeing missionary work, as Dr Warzeski points out, not only as satisfying their own spiritual needs but also as a means of achieving professional satisfaction. Clearly they could speak Arabic, clearly their work gave them access to a wide range of Egyptian society and clearly their medical work, like Lucie Duff Gordon's first aid, was greatly appreciated and gave them an *entrée* to the world around them in which women played a far more vital role than one would guess from even such notable male experts as Edward Lane and Karl Klunzinger. Like the Misses Muir Mackenzie and Irby the American missionaries also left a lasting educational legacy, even though only within minority Christian communities.

As Janet Starkey notes, 'orientalism' is generally seen as a male construct but similar limitations apply to several of the women included here. Their travels were geographically restricted, by and large excluding areas remote from the Nile valley such as Egypt's Eastern Desert that she writes about. Most of the women included here were like ships passing in the night; nevertheless listen to Tennyson's Ulysses in old age talking to his son Telemechus: 'I am a part of all that I have met;/Yet all experience is an arch wherethro'/Gleams that untravelled world…' One longs to gather up all these women in a harim, with their water pipes and letter writing equipment and sips of tea or coffee, listen to their experiences and hear them echo the old man: 'How dull it is to pause, to make an end …'

2. Travelling to Post: Lady Liston, an Ambassadress in Constantinople

Deborah Manley

Our knowledge of the hazards and pleasures of the journey to the East – and particularly to Turkey – in the eighteenth and early nineteenth centuries – comes typically from women, and particularly from the wives of four British ambassadors. Britain was well served by the ambassadresses – as the wives of ambassadors were known – at the Ottoman Porte at this time. They included four women who stand out as personalities in their own right. The best known are the two Marys (Lady Mary Wortley Montagu and Lady Elgin), but Lady Liston and Lady Canning deserve more attention than they receive.

The most famous was Lady Mary Wortley Montagu. Surprisingly when one thinks of her impact, she was only in Constantinople itself for twelve months in 1717–18. She travelled East in 1717 through the Balkans and her letters – published and republished over the years – have fixed early eighteenth century Constantinople into our minds – and the minds of her successors who had apparently read them.[1] Also well known – from her notorious life and her letters home to her mother (published in 1926) – was Lady Elgin (1777–1855), wife of Lord Elgin, purchaser of the marbles. The Elgins lived in Constantinople from 1799 to 1803.[2] The longest serving ambassadress, Lady Canning, was barely eighteen when she married the widowed Stratford Canning, nephew of the Foreign Secretary, who was twenty years her senior and had already served four years in Turkey. He returned, with her, as ambassador in 1825, served there off and on and finally left from their final tour in 1857 when she was 51. She was

---

[1] Lady Mary Wortley Montagu, *The Travel letters of Mary Wortley Montagu* (London, 1763).

[2] Lady Elgin, *Letters of Nary Nisbet of Dirleton* (London, 1926).

usually at his side and hers is a fascinating life – including her entanglements with Florence Nightingale. Her importance to the ambassador, Stratford Canning, is unquestionable.[3]

The least known of this quartet – probably one of the oldest foreign women in the East at the time – Lady Liston (1751–1828), had aspirations to become a latter day Lady Mary. Henrietta Marchant was born in Antigua in the Caribbean in 1751, the eighth of thirteen children. In 1796, at the age of 45, she married Mr Liston (later Sir Robert) in Glasgow where she had come to live with an uncle and aunt. Robert was 54 years old, and recently returned from serving three years as ambassador to the Porte. Her accounts of their posting to Philadelphia, only thirteen years after the end of the American War of Independence, are an important historic record of early post-colonial America. The portrait of her in Washington, by Gilbert Stuart, shows the pleasing, strong face of a middle-aged woman, then newly married. In 1804, after their years in the United States and postings in Europe, the Listons returned to Scotland and virtual retirement, until, in 1812, he was recalled and again posted to Constantinople, and she, then 61, sailed with him. The Listons travelled east by sea, took one long home leave in 1815–17 and eventually retired to Millburn Towers, their house near Edinburgh, in 1821 to enjoy, as Sir Robert wrote, 'the evening of their days'.[4]

Henrietta was clearly a self-assured, outgoing, tough lady, interested in life around her – the sort of woman whom embassy staff laugh about but also appreciate; a woman who communicated comfortably with those around her, was interested in and observant of both social life and the political background of the countries where she travelled.

She left a wonderful legacy. In the National Library of Scotland are her letters, writings, journal notes and much else. The American letters were used in 1954 by B. Perkins in an article entitled 'A Diplomat's Wife in Philadelphia: The Letters of Henrietta Liston, 1796–1800'.[5] Since then nothing appears to have been published and they remain an almost unplumbed resource.

Lady Liston, a well-considered botanist and plant collector, sent plants to the omnipresent Sir Joseph Banks. Sir Robert described her as 'somewhat of a Botanist, and a very great florist and gardener' who encouraged others to collect seeds and bulbs for her in their travels. In Scotland she made an American garden and an Eastern garden for which she asked travellers and friends to send plants. In January 1815 she wrote in Constantinople:

---

[3] Stanley Lane Poole, *The Life of Stratford Canning* (London, 1888).

[4] Liston papers, National Library of Scotland, various mss indicated as NLS.

[5] *William and Mary Historical Journal* (Williamsburg), 592 and 596.

Our Garden has bloomed with flowers of various kinds particularly with fine Bulbs – and I have been enabled to produce – from the open Air – a Bouquet of showy flowers on the Marble-table of the Dining Room every Tuesday – which is our Publick Day.[6]

The Listons had to spend nearly a year waiting in London for their order to depart for the East. Sir Robert, – whose quiet humour I came increasingly to enjoy, as I read his letters – wrote on March 21st 1812: '…my wife and I have glided imperceptibly into the idle habits of the idle inhabitants.'

On April 8th 1812 they set off at last from Portsmouth, into bad weather. Their journey was carefully recorded from embarkation to arrival at the end of June, by Henrietta herself, and by members of the embassy: Brigadier Sir Robert Wilson (who was travelling on into Russia and whose diaries show he enjoyed a good bit of gossip alongside important matters of state) and the young diplomat William Turner, who later travelled widely in the Levant and Egypt. Wilson reported stormy seas accompanied by dirty weather – 'all passengers sick … heavy swell and frequent squalls…' They were off Cadiz before there was a mild day, and then they were delayed by storms for a week. Even in the Mediterranean in early May the weather was such that they saw little of Mrs Liston except at meals, but Robert Wilson wrote: 'she proves herself to merit the opinion I had formed of her understanding and kind disposition.' They beat their way with fresh gales and very little progress to Palermo, where rain poured all day from black skies, and even when they departed on 20 May, although the weather was very fine, there was a foul wind.[7]

Henrietta had until now considered herself a good sailor. In 1796 on their voyage to America, despite the high seas, her only real complaint to her uncle in Glasgow – to whom she wrote regularly – was not about the 'gale more severe than had ever been seen by any person on board', though it concerned them that her loss might bring sorrow to them, but that one of their footmen had the smallpox – 'the most inconvenient disease he could have had.' She was a kind-hearted woman, so we must assume he survived. On that journey she 'gained credit with the officers by being the best female sailor any of them ever saw.'[8]

Now she wrote miserably of 'the horrid Bay of Biscay … during which I was very unwell.' At last they sailed into the Grand Harbour at Valetta – one of the greatest experiences of the Mediterranean – 'early enough to enjoy the view of its magnificence. I had never witnessed anything so grand as the prospect of the city, when we coasted down its port,' recorded the young embassy secretary, William Turner.[9] The Liston party were hospitably received by Sir Hildebrand

---

[6] NLS 5708.f.7.

[7] Sir Robert Wilson, *Private Diary of Travels, Personal Services and Public Events*, 2 vols (London, 1861) I, 29.

[8] B.Perkins, 596–7.

[9] William Turner, *Travels in the Levant*, 2 vols (London, 1820) I, 26.

Oakes, commander-in-chief and civil commissioner of Malta, then only a decade under British rule. Henrietta had interesting comments on the interior of the Palace of the Knights of Malta where they stayed. On May 28th they sailed on to Greece, eventually reaching the entrance to the Dardanelles on June 12th 1812.

A message was sent to advise the acting ambassador, Stratford Canning, of their coming. Their ship anchored near the supposed plain of Troy, and while they waited for word from Constantinople, Sir Robert Wilson and the other single men went off to explore the Troad. A day later the Listons followed: he on a finely caparisoned horse provided by the Turkish governor, she 'in a little car, drawn by two buffaloes', as she had not *yet* learned to ride à la Turque – that is astride rather than side-saddle. Wilson wrote admiringly: 'I think she has done right to brave all the inconveniences, but if she sleeps where Captain Warren and I did she will certainly leave the greater part of her skin behind.' He suffered greatly from what he called 'my Asiatic acquaintance' or 'our troublesome adherents'.[10] Henrietta appeared seldom bothered by them.

She noted everything they passed: the scenes of the Trojan wars, the turbans crowning the graves in the Turkish burial grounds, the remains of a Greek church, the storks that bring happiness to the house on which they nest. The local Aga offered a delicious breakfast, eaten from spoons of painted wood, their hands washed with water poured from a ewer. Mounted on an ass, she climbed to see Hector's tomb and the citadel of Troy – though she had doubts about their veracity from her own readings. They rode on to the few remaining buildings of Alexandria Troas – which had seriously deteriorated since Mr Liston had been there some years earlier. The great officers of state came to welcome them with gifts and festivities, and their arrival caused much excitement. 'We were regarded,' she recognised, 'as a Chinese Ambassador and his wife would be in an English village.'

One cool evening they began to be rowed up the Dardanelles – their Greek oarsmen trying to out-row the Turks – reflecting, she thought, the near hatred with which they regarded 'their haughty conquerors'. At each stop there was more feasting and celebrations. The Listons found the meals extravagantly generous, but Henrietta felt happier when she learned that 'the leftovers were given to the Poor.'[11]

At last Constantinople rose ahead, with its beautiful buildings enlivened by 'the intermixture of Gardens and fine trees – as all Turkish situations are'. Henrietta's descriptions are lively and knowledgeable, written up in fair copy from her first impressions. On June 28th at Pera, where the embassy palace lay, a great crowd were assembled, and she was carried to the British palace in a sedan chair. Stratford Canning (still only 25 years old and having carried the

---

[10] Wilson I, 90.
[11] NLS 5709.f.32.

responsibilities of the embassy for almost two years) was able to record: 'joyfully delivered the charge of the mission which had been to the last degree irksome and embarrassing' to his successor.[12]

In any institution like a foreign embassy there are internal jokes and anecdotes. Henrietta, stout, in her sixties and somewhat exuberant, was bound to provide some. Sir Robert Wilson tells how, early in their time in Constantinople, the Grand Seigneur lost his only male child. The dragoman reported that as he had four wives already pregnant, the loss was not irreparable.

Mrs Liston misheard and repeated, 'Four wives petulant!'

'*Pregnant,* madam, *pregnant,*' Liston said.

'God bless me!' shrieked Her Excellency, 'who could have thought of that? I am sure petulant was a more reasonable supposition. Four wives *pregnant* !' The phenomenon seemed to press upon her mind and Wilson suspected he would shortly hear of a visit to the Seraglio.[13]

As with all travellers the first months in the new country bring the most surprises and the greatest impact. Thus it was in 1813 that Henrietta recorded most of her impressions. However, the Listons were virtually imprisoned by the plague for some months, though making one excursion in a showy barge up the Bosphorus. She was delighted, finding everything 'so gay, beautiful and interesting … like a succession of fine Lakes, its sides ornamented by Fairy Palaces of the Sultans, Gardens, arbours … under the shade of which the Turks delight to sit, and the view terminated by wooded Hills. The summer houses and kiosks were gilded and painted in the gayest manner.' (At one end of each long building she noted the white or gilded lattice windows of the women.) Still rather gay than melancholy were the burial grounds – both public and private. The public grounds contained thickly planted cypresses and the coloured turbans of the departed; the private were surrounded by fine painted or gilded railings.[14]

At the entrance to the Black Sea lay a dozen ships of the Turkish fleet. Henrietta described the strength and power of the navy; the Capitan Pasha – the Ottoman admiral Kusraw Mohammed, was supposed to be partial to the English, having lived much with them in Egypt in 1801, on the joint expedition against the French. He invited the Listons to visit him on his 100-gun flag ship. While Mr Liston and the Pasha discussed business, Henrietta was able to provide a splendid description of sofas, cushions and embroidered pillows, gilded chairs, marble tables and silk curtains – all the colours of the rainbow – and much else that adorned the Capitan Pasha's quarters.[15]

---

[12] Lane Poole I, 175.
[13] Wilson I, 131.
[14] NLS 5709.f.32.
[15] NLS 5709.f.37.

Henrietta enthusiastically described the preparations for Liston's first public audience with the Grand Vizier and later with the Grand Seigneur – the Sultan himself. On the first occasion, on July 30th, Wilson's party were leaving Pera for Russia 'amidst a scene of comic disorder' occasioned by the bustle of his departure and preparations for Mr Liston's visit.[16]

Henrietta wrote not only of the grand occasions. She wrote of many other matters: of the labouring poor 'on whom the Sultan was an affliction'; of the plague which raged with progressive violence beyond the gates of the British palace so that not even the servants could go out of the gates until severe winter weather dispersed its 'dreadful ravages' – and the garden which provided their only exercise. Once they were freed from confinement, she wrote of government and punishment, of the janissaries, of the customs of Ramadhan (the Muslim month of fasting), of the lights of the minarets, of the dogs with litters of puppies that lay in the streets so that it was difficult not to trip over them, and about the birds of prey which cleaned the streets; she watched the checking of the market weights and commented on the heating systems for the Turkish winter. She commented upon the relationship of the Turks to their slaves – some Serbian, some black, some Christian, many Muslim – and noted that the slaves often achieved high positions in society, one senior Turk having a black wife. She wrote about the term 'Sultana' and she wrote of the funerals of the different religious groups.

One of the hazards of life in Constantinople, with its many wooden buildings, was fire. The English traveller Thomas Legh passing through Constantinople early in 1818 witnessed 'almost daily occasions … of considerable conflagrations, as well as most extraordinary sights that usually attract the attention of a stranger: - the exposure of a dead body in the streets, naked and decapitated.' It lay near their hotel for three days guarded by janissaries 'to keep the numerous ravenous dogs at bay.'[17]

On October 5th 1814 the British palace at Pera itself was threatened by fire and Henrietta (having been dressed by her English maid) went out to find the house and garden illuminated by flames from the blazing houses in the streets beyond their gates. She returned to her room for her jewel box, writing box and money and joined the concourse of people in the palace garden. Fire engines were present, but not being used.

'Why?' she asked.

'Because no money had been given,' was the reply.

'I could,' she wrote, 'almost have seen them bastinadoed with pleasure.'

She later discovered that only once payment was made would the firemen

---

[16] Wilson I, 412.

[17] Thomas Legh in Dr William Macmichael's *Journey from Moscow to Constantinople* (London, 1819).

work and that even the Grand Seigneur's power of immediate harassment and death could not be exercised on such occasions. Indeed the firemen would even abuse him to his face.[18]

Dr John Griffiths travelling in the region in 1805 also described this ancient custom. The Grand Seigneur was expected to attend fires to distribute money and 'excite the efforts of the firemen'. They wait, Griffiths noted, 'for the money to come – appear zealous – receive a gratuity – relax in their efforts – and are again stimulated by a present.' (Interestingly, in 1666 the King of England went himself to distribute monies to the workers trying to defeat the Great Fire of London.) 'The women, under pretence of bewailing misfortune, loudly exclaim against ministers and even the Sultan himself.' Griffiths wondered whether some fires were set with hopes of redress in cases of peculiar grievance.[19]

The Listons visited the dervish community and watched them 'whirling round with such constancy and velocity as often to fall to insensibility.' They visited a factory where she watched children printing the muslins, 'overlooked by old persons'. They went to view the gathering of the pilgrims bound for Mecca – 'in circumstances peculiarly pleasing to the Sultan' for it was the first pilgrimage since the holy cities of Mecca and Madina had been returned to the Sultanate by the governor of Egypt, Muhammad Ali, after their possession by the militant reform movement of the Wahhabis, whom Henrietta defined as 'a sort of Unitarians to the Mohametan faith'. They met Muhammad Ali's son, come to Constantinople for the occasion – 'an ill-looking youth,' she thought. At the head of the procession was an old man who had been the first Turkish ambassador to England, and was now responsible for the upkeep of the 3–4,000 poor pilgrims on the journey.[20]

On a trip to Asia Minor in June 1813, Henrietta took the opportunity to go to a public bath house – Lady Mary Wortley Montagu's description in her mind. She found the bathers 'strolling and sitting and lolling in every corner – in buff.' The whole scene was strange to her eyes – but picturesque and fine. She was urged to join in but found the heat suffocating, and, shy of the attention she attracted, was 'impatient to get out with all my Clothes upon my back.'[21]

In August 1813 – as Wilson had surmised she would – Henrietta visited the *harim* of a Minister with the embassy dragoman's wife as interpreter. The ladies greatly admired 'the form which her Corsets gave to the Breast of her gown' while Henrietta regretted that their mode of dress with no support 'spoilt their shapes'. They were intrigued by her long gloves – 'and the delicacy of the French leather astonished them very much.' Always a careful observer, Henrietta

---

[18] NLS 5708.f.1.
[19] Dr J. Griffiths, *Travels in the East, Armenia and Arabia* (London, 1805), 82.
[20] NLS 5709.f.55–58.
[21] NLS 5709.f.70.

recorded the other ladies' dress and decoration, details of the apartments she was guided through and the dishes served to her – of which she both enthused and criticised. The Minister's wife gratified her by telling her that 'many good Turks thought the English the best <u>Allies</u> Turkey could have. They had always found the English upright and honest and not telling lies.'[22]

In January 1814 two events provided much interest. On January 18th, being the Queen's birthday, they held a ball at the British palace. 'The late happy Peace having united all Parties … our large and numerous apartments were, for the first time, nearly filled. There were upwards of three hundred people … of twenty different nations … a mixture of very extraordinary figures and costumes.' On the very next day 'a scene very different indeed' absorbed her attention for several pages of her journal. Doctor Lorenzo, who had been physician to the Seraglio, was 'cruelly' murdered. His body was found on the hill ascending to the Arsenal and Henrietta posed many questions about the implications of this tragedy.[23]

Henrietta had been well aware of such a threat to foreigners. In bidding farewell to Sir Robert Wilson a month after their arrival at Pera, she said that, although she loved him, she was delighted he was leaving as she constantly feared that from his wanderings in the city 'I should bring her home the plague, or be brought home with a dagger through my body for trespassing on Turkish property.'[24]

In October 1815 the Listons journeyed back to England on leave, returning nearly two years later. Her journal of this journey starts with words with which we can all sympathise: 'we were so entirely engrossed by business and by the painful duty of taking leave of our friends … that we were at last obliged to depart precipitately, forgetting a thousand things.'

Henrietta would have liked to tarry at the island of Lesbos to see where Sappho lived but 'it seemed to be my Husband's maxim to proceed expeditiously.' They paused at Smyrna to be entertained by Consul Werry and sailed on to Athens past fertile islands. Skio, she noted, supplied a great deal of mastic to the Grand Seigneur that the ladies of the seraglio chewed as 'a sweetener of the breath'. They sailed past Delos at night and she regretted not being able to say she had touched the birthplace of Apollo. Near Sunion, the scene of 'Falconer's beautiful Poem, which makes generally a part of a Seaman's library', she read an officer's copy 'on the very spot as she looked up at the remaining 15 Columbs (sic) of the temple of Minerva'.[25] One can imagine Henrietta reading Falconer's words as the ship passed the Aegean islands:

---

[22] NLS 5709.f.72.
[23] NLS 20.1.1215.
[24] Wilson I, 134.
[25] NLS 5710 *passim.*

Then tower'd the masts; the canvas swelled on high
And waving streamers floated in the sky.
Thus the rich vessel moves in trim array
Like some fair virgin on her bridal day;
Thus like a swan she cleaves the wat'ry plain
The pride and wonder of the Aegean main.[26]

In Athens the Listons were welcomed by Monsieur Lusier (who had been employed as Lord Elgin's draughtsman and in taking down the marbles) and Monsieur Lagothete accompanied by a Band – of, punned Henrietta, 'Banditti' – of the Governor's Albanian Guard who strolled before them on foot to do them honour. Along the road Henrietta recognised familiar classical sites, though becoming much fatigued by riding à la Turque (astride) – and wearing Turkish drawers. So much had been said of Athens that she only described its effect on herself. When they visited the Acropolis she commented on its beauty 'injured only by the <u>Patreism</u> or <u>Selfishism</u> of a former British Ambassador' that had removed one of the Caryatides – and, one may assume, some 'Marbles'. The exotic pleasures of their stay were added to by their hostess, Madame Lagothete – a handsome woman who appeared from the beginning to the end of the day in what Henrietta described as 'the full ancient Greek costume.'[27]

From Athens they sailed along the coast in an increasingly frustrating effort to catch up with the ship which had carried them to Greece but which had gone ahead while they were in Athens. At night they slept on the ground, though on mattresses, and only as well 'as the vermin would allow us'. They were stuck at Corinth waiting for their ship and, for once, Henrietta sounded a bit querulous: 'the wine was impregnated with resin – so that a stranger cannot drink it'; Corinth was 'a most miserable dull place'; their landlord was 'an Italian rogue grafted upon a Greek one'. They eventually escaped but contrary winds, occasional squalls and the strong current slowed their progress, and Henrietta was not sure 'whether we had been drowned, the fame of being lost on Classic

---

[26] William Falconer, Canto I: The Shipwreck, 1762. See James Silk Buckingham, *Autobiography* (London, 1855). The poem was unfamiliar to me but by serendipity I soon after read Buckingham's *Autobiography*. An erudite sea captain he also kept Falconer's 'Shipwreck' in his kitbag and explained how the poem 'accurately enumerates all the characteristic traits' of Athens, Corinth, Troy, the islands and all the prominent points connected with mythology, history and poetry 'undyingly connected with each' (Buckingham I, 389). Buckingham wrote that he never read the poem 'with such intense enjoyment as while sailing through the Greek Archipelago, with the very places he so graphically describes passing successively before my eyes.' To enjoy it to its best, Buckingham 'repaired to the maintop, and there, alone, and absorbed with the subject, enjoyed it free from interruption.' *The Shipwreck* introduces the reader in poetic form to the masts, yards, sails and rigging of a merchant ship and how they functioned, or did not function, in an Aegean storm.
[27] NLS 5710, 24.10.1815.

ground would have entirely consoled our friends.' Yet, despite discomforts, Henrietta described the beauty of the area with enthusiasm: 'the Gulf rendered enchanting by the variety of shades and forms reflected in the waters', and always she was able to enthuse about the flora. At Patras, all the consuls talked of 'following the present *rage* for *excavation*' and the Austrian consul showed off his trophies. At last reaching Corfu they expected to enjoy the comforts of the Governor General's house. It was not to be. 'The late unfortunate King of Sweden' (who her husband had known as a boy) was there – accompanied by 'a little <u>Peasant Mistress</u>' – 'which circumstance had banished from the Government House all the Ladies of the island' and so they soon sailed on to Naples, where they had to undertake quarantine before they could return to Europe proper, although this was shortened partly by 'consideration for Mr Liston's rank'.[28]

Liston's rank was to be increased during their time in Britain for Mr Liston became Sir Robert – and she Lady Liston. Unfortunately her account of their return journey in July 1817 seems to have suffered a watery fate and is virtually unreadable. But it is clear that, once their ship had tacked its way up the Golden Horn to the mooring, past 'one continuous scene of enchantment' and reached anchor and their 'family' of friends waiting to accompany them to the Embassy, she was happy to be home in Turkey again. 'Our Palace appeared beautiful' and Bartle Frere, who had acted in Sir Robert's place, had beautified the garden. In the next few months there was 'an inundation of Travellers – the Mania which infects the English is as strong as ever,' she noted, 'and their numbers are greater than when the Continent was shut and the Levant alone open to them.' She rejoiced, however, that, by taking leave at that time they had avoided the visit of Caroline, Princess of Wales, who had been 'an expensive and troublesome guest.'

They spent three more years in Constantinople on their final tour of duty and, in 1818, Sir Robert, describing their roles in a letter to the author Jane Porter, sister of the well-travelled artist Sir Robert Ker Porter, wrote: 'Lady Liston <u>employs</u> herself, as a good Diplomatic Consort might do, in keeping up a friendly intercourse with all mankind; and her <u>amusement</u> is the management and amelioration of the garden, where utility is mixed with ornament and which is fast advancing to beauty. <u>I</u> find sufficient occupation in patching and palliating and endeavouring to prevent mischief.' What a splendid description of the role of an ambassador. He added that they were both 'blessed with health not inferior to that of our younger neighbours.'

When the Listons finally left Turkey in July 1820 they were sent off with splendid gifts from the Sultan: Sir Robert with a box handsomely set with diamonds, she with four superb cashmere shawls. At last, having divested

---

[28] NLS 5710 5710 *passim.*

themselves of 'lingering responsibility' they were accompanied to the shore – of a 'never-to-be-forgotten beautiful Bosphorus' – and seen off by not only their 'embassy family' but also many others. She looked back at 'the House, the Garden, every local object in and around our dwelling – all made more interesting by the painful idea of seeing them for the last time.'[29] Some sadness she may also have felt that they were going into retirement for the last time – though still she only a vigorous seventy and he not quite eighty years old.

---

[29] NLS 5712, 7.7.1820.

3. Two Feisty Ladies in the Levant: Princess Caroline and Lady Craven

Charles Plouviez

In the spring of 1815, while Napoleon was on his way to Waterloo, two rather naughty English ladies met for tea in Genoa. They were as different in appearance as in character; and although they were spending two hours together, they did not much like one another. Yet they had quite a lot in common. The elder, remaining at 64 a tall and elegant English aristocrat, was the twice-widowed Margravine of Anspach, formerly Elizabeth Craven, described in a recent book as 'a famous beauty, traveller and dramatist whose lifestyle generated almost non-stop scandal.'[1] She had seen two of her plays produced at Drury Lane and one printed by Horace Walpole before the series of scandals which led to separation from her first husband drove her abroad in 1783. After her husband died, she had married the Margrave and returned to live in England, but Queen Charlotte refused to receive her as the Margravine. So, when she was widowed for the second time, she chose to live chiefly abroad.

Her hostess, at 47, short, plain and dumpy and with a comic German accent, was Caroline, Princess of Wales. Loathed by her husband the Prince Regent from the moment they met, she had been in 1805 the victim of a demeaning if inconclusive investigation into an allegation that she had had an illegitimate child. But it was only in 1814, after the Prince refused her access to their daughter, that she left the country.

On the day they met for tea, the Princess of Wales had her Mediterranean travels and her worst scandal still to come. Elizabeth Craven, as she is best known, had hers behind her. It would be pleasant to speculate that over their tea Elizabeth advised Caroline on where to shop in Constantinople and what to

---

[1] Frances Wilson, *The Courtesan's Revenge* (London, Faber, 2003), 36.

Elizabeth (Berkeley), Margravine of Anspach [previously Lady Craven], painted by Ozias Humphry, ca. 1780–83. Published courtesy of the National Portrait Gallery.

wear in Athens, but it is unlikely. They met solely because Craven was trying to trace her youngest son, Keppel, who with his close friend Sir William Gell had been the Princess's chamberlains until she had left Naples. Caroline was unable to help.

Both ladies were well travelled in the conventional parts of Europe, and indeed only about a quarter of Craven's book, *A Journey through the Crimea to Constantinople. In a series of letters from the right honourable Elizabeth Lady Craven to His Serene Highness the Margrave of Brandebourg, Anspach, and Bareith* covers

Queen Caroline painted by James Lonsdale, 1820. Published courtesy of the National Portrait Gallery.

ASTENE territory. And Caroline was to spend some years in Italy before embarking on her fateful tour of the Near East. But since both ladies visited Constantinople and Athens, it is on these areas that I want to concentrate.

Back in 1783, Lady Craven had fled to France with her infant son Keppel. After two years in Paris, she parked Keppel safely and went on her tour. Her route was well publicised, so that Horace Walpole was able to warn his friend Sir Horace Mann, the British minister in Florence, of her approach, adding 'she has, I fear, been *infinitamente* indiscreet; but what is that to you or me? She is very pretty, and is good-natured to the greatest degree; has not a grain of malice or mischief … and never has been an enemy but to herself.'[2]

Craven travelled at leisure through France and Italy, to Vienna, Warsaw and St Petersburg, where she called on Catherine the Great before turning south to visit Moscow and the Crimea. None of this is very remarkable: the aristocracy had its own European community, and she was just one aristocrat calling on others of her kind in similar courts and palaces.

It is only when she takes ship across the Black Sea to Constantinople that the tone of her letters changes. At this date, western women, apart from ambassadors' wives, did not travel in the Ottoman Empire – indeed, Craven was the first woman after Lady Mary Wortley Montagu to publish an account of such a tour. Travel everywhere was arduous and slow; fleas and lice were the least of the dangers; robbers and epidemics the worst. But the Ottoman Empire was not just another country, but a totally strange culture. And Craven, though an intelligent and sensitive woman, had absorbed every racist stereotype her culture had to offer.

Fortunately for her, on her arrival at the Bosphorus, Elizabeth was met by servants of the French ambassador, the Comte de Choiseul-Gouffier, who brought her to the Palais de France in Pera, near today's Hilton Hotel, and with a view across the Golden Horn similar to that sketched at about the same date by Thomas Hope. She admired the splendour of the city, and especially its trees, and from Choiseul-Gouffier's windows, she says, 'we had a large telescope, and saw the Ottoman splendour very distinctly,' including the Sultan sitting on his silver sofa.[3]

But the Turks were something else. Craven, who had written earlier, 'you know, Sir, I have no English prejudices,'[4] dutifully recites the lessons she might have learned from Mozart's *Die Entführung*. Turks are lazy, fat, stupid, incapable of running anything and easily fooled by their wives, who use their segregation and their veils to intrigue against their husbands in perfect safety. 'I think I never saw a country where women may enjoy so much liberty, and free from all reproach,' she writes, with a touch of what sounds like jealousy. But her contempt for the men is boundless. 'I saw a Turk the other day,' she continues, 'lying on a cushion, striking slowly an iron which he was shaping into an horse-shoe, his pipe in his mouth all the time … Perhaps, Sir, it is lucky for Europe that the Turks are idle and ignorant – the immense power this empire might have, were it only peopled by the industrious and ambitious, would make it the mistress of the world …'[5]

---

[2] quoted in *Dictionary of National Biography*, 'Anspach, Elizabeth, Margravine'.

[3] Elizabeth Craven, *A Journey through the Crimea to Constantinople* (London, 1789), Letter XLVI, 103–4.

[4] Elizabeth Craven, *Letters from the Right Honourable Lady Craven… during her travels…* (London, 1814) Letter XVII, 43.

[5] Elizabeth Craven, *A Journey through the Crimea to Constantinople*, Letter XLVI, 205–6.

She is equally unimpressed by Aya Sofia, then a mosque, where she admits the dome is 'well worth seeing' but complains about the 'capitals of Turkish architecture' and deplores that 'some shabby lamps, hung irregularly, are the only expence the Mahometans permit themselves, as a proof of their respect for the Deity or his Prophet.' What really impresses her about mosques is how easily they too could be used for purposes of intrigue: 'a figure, wrapped up like a mummy, can easily kneel down by another without being suspected, and mutter in a whisper any sort of thing.'[6] Here, surely, we hear Craven the dramatist speaking.

The first volume of the Comte's *Voyage Pittoresque de la Grèce* had appeared in 1782, and he was the ideal host for Elizabeth Craven – knowledgeable, civilised and rich. He was able not only to ensure her admittance to the women's quarters of a Turkish house – something that was becoming a regular outing for European women, whose menfolk were barred from its mysteries – but also to advise her on her visit to Greece and to provide the frigate *Tarleton* to take her by way of Naxos to Andiparos to visit the stalactite cave, where he persuaded her to become the first woman to make the 300-foot descent.[7]

From Andiparos, Craven sailed to Piraeus and visited Athens where she did the accustomed round of the time, commenting on what were then called the Temple of Minerva, Temple of Theseus, Lanthorn of Diogenes, Temple of the Winds and Temple of Jupiter Olympus. She describes them in the vein of an eighteenth-century dilettante; remarking for instance on her first sight of 'the superb, the beautiful Temple of Theseus' that the architecture was 'simple and grand – proportioned with majesty and grace; it has stood to this day an eternal monument of the good taste of the ancients.'[8]

She was tempted to pick up a piece of the Parthenon sculpture lying on the ground, but Choiseul-Gouffier had been negotiating for a year for permission to remove a fragment to Constantinople:

> The sailors were prepared with cranes, and every thing necessary to convey this beautiful relic on board the Tarleton; when – after the governor of the citadel, a Turk, had received us with great politeness, he took M. de Truguet aside, and told him, unless he chose to endanger his life, he must give up the thoughts of touching any thing…[9]

She thought the Parthenon pediment sculptures were 'executed in the most masterly manner; there is a female figure holding the reins to drive two fiery steeds, which seem to snort and prance in marble.' And, anticipating Elgin, she proposes to her correspondent the Margrave that the Austrian Emperor could

---

[6] *Ibid.,* Letter XLVIII, 217, 218.
[7] *Ibid.,* Letter LIII, 246 *et seq.,* Letter LIV. 249.
[8] *Ibid.,* Letter LIV, 254.
[9] *Ibid.,* Letter LV, 256.

'take advantage of the desire the Porte has to oblige him, in order to collect the fragments of the sculpture of the Temple of Minerva, to preserve them as examples to this or rising generations, and as models for the ingenious workman to study from.'[10] Eventually, Choiseul-Gouffier did succeed in acquiring the metope and section of frieze now in the Louvre. Meanwhile, Craven had retired to the baths, where, she says, 'I think I never saw so many fat women at once together, nor fat ones so fat as these.'[11]

Princess Caroline was getting pretty fat by the time she embarked on her long voyage of 1815. Unlike Craven, she did not write her memoirs; her only personal contribution comes in a brief itinerary she prepared subsequently for her lawyers and a letter from Tunis (her first stop after Sicily) to her former chamberlain and mentor on classical affairs, Sir William Gell. But immediately, the difference between the two women is apparent: Caroline has none of Craven's prejudices.

'The ship sails extremely well and I shall embark as tomorrow morning to go directly to Athens,' she writes in her quaint English, 'six weeks I shall remain in the Shore and then to Constantinople, where I shall certainly remain more than a month. I shall then go to Smyrna, St. Jean d'Acre, Jerusalem, and only return I do not know when…' This letter is important as showing her attitude to both the antiquities and the people she is visiting. She tells Gell, 'I have been three times in the Seraglio and received most kindly. I have seen the dancing of the Country and their very fine dinners. The Bey's son is a very fine young man … In short I could write a volume to you about all what I have seen here. I am living a perfect enchantment. The dear Arabians and Turks are quite darlings.'[12]

Alas, Caroline had to leave her darlings somewhat hurriedly. Her visit was curtailed by the arrival of a British naval vessel threatening to bombard the town if the Bey did not surrender his European slaves. As she reports it to Gell, 'I … had the pleasure to release great many slaves, before when the English fleet arrived which came only a week later than I.' And she adds, 'I am quite in astonishment that all the wonderful curiosities of Carthage, Utica, Savonny, Udinna never have been taken much notice of.'[13]

So, although contemporaries were much more interested in the future Queen's shipboard adultery than her sightseeing, and her most recent biographers are contemptuous of her travels,[14] she shows both more tolerance for the local people than Craven and an appreciation of the antiquities, no doubt learned from Keppel and Gell.

---

[10] *Ibid.*, Letter LV, 261–2.

[11] *Ibid.*, Letter LVI, 263–4.

[12] Princess Caroline, letter to Sir William Gell (21 April 1816), Derbyshire Record Office, D3287.

[13] *Ibid.*

[14] Flora Fraser, *The Unruly Queen: the life of Queen Caroline* (London, Macmillan, 1996).

Accounts of Caroline's travels are abundant but mostly fictitious. The only ones with any claim to authenticity are the brief diary of a naval lieutenant who travelled with her, and a volume purporting to be by Louise Demont, the maid who gave evidence against her at her so-called trial. In spite of its dodgy provenance, it seems fairly accurate. And her itinerary is well documented: from Tunis she sailed to Piraeus, took in Athens and Corinth, then by the Aegean and the supposed site of Troy to Constantinople and back round the coast of Asia Minor to reach a grand finale in Jerusalem.

She spent only a fortnight in Greece, but Demont says they visited the Acropolis, the Theseum, the hill of the Muses, Pnyx, Areopagus, Philopappus Monument, both theatres, the 'lantern of Demosthenes,' Hadrian's arch, the Temple of Jupiter and the stadium, as well as such dubious out-of-town sites as the house of Plato. Her account of the Theseum is vastly different from Craven's: 'it is the best preserved monument, not only in the city, but in the world. It consists of thirty-six columns [*nearly right, there are 34*] of white marble, of the Doric order; the columns are eighteen feet in height, and are ornamented with bas-reliefs of the exploits of Theseus: at this time the temple is converted into a church, for the use of the Greeks, and is dedicated to St. George, their protecting saint.'[15] This is not just picturesque description, but a sound architectural account consistent with what a clever Swiss girl might have picked up from a well-informed mistress.

Like any travelling princess, Caroline also had a social programme. Demont gives a lengthy account of their visit to the dancing dervishes in the Tower of the Winds, declaring, 'I was so overcome by terror, that I involuntarily seized hold of a gentleman who was by my side, and trembled from head to foot.'[16]

But Craven and Demont agree about Greek music and dancing. Craven had reported: 'a more stupid performance as a dance I never saw… A woman… gets up and with a handkerchief in one hand, waves it about in a languid manner; with the other she holds the hand of a second, who leads a third, and so on … the music is as dull and uniform as her steps, which like her eyes, never lose the ground.'[17] And Demont says: 'their manner of dancing is insipid to the last degree … The male part of the creation are never allowed to join in the dance, which merely consists in one lady giving her hand to another, and turning her. Their music consists, without any variation, in lá, lá, lá, lá, lá, lá, and lá, lá, lá.'[18]

At Corinth, there being few antiquities to view, the Princess visited a seraglio. She returned to Athens and sailed from Piraeus for Constantinople by way of

---

[15] Louise Demont, *Voyages and Travels of Her Majesty, Caroline Queen of Great Britain, etc.* (London, Jones & Co, 1821), 22.

[16] Louise Demont, *ibid.,* 25.

[17] Elizabeth Craven, *op. cit.,* Letter LVI, 264–5.

[18] Louise Demont, *op. cit.,* 31.

Troy, where Demont laments, 'there is no longer a stone to be seen of its once proud edifices, and its site is an unbroken plain, planted with olive trees. We twice passed the Scamander, which formerly crossed the city. At a trifling distance is New Troy, built by Alexander the Great. The town is not, in any way, remarkable.'[19] No doubt the Princess was well informed on the site of Troy (the wrong site, as Schliemann would later prove), because Gell had written a famous book about it.

Constantinople when she reached it was something of a disappointment. 'On the day of our arrival,' says Demont, 'we disembarked, and went to reside at the spacious palace of the British ambassador [the ambassador, Robert Liston, was on leave, perhaps luckily for him: see previous essay]. When within the city, it appears far from beautiful, owing to the narrowness and dirtiness of the streets. Her Royal Highness, her lady of honor, my sister, and myself, went up in a sort of car on two wheels, drawn by oxen, which is the best equipage the country affords …' She adds, wrongly I assume, that 'the Mosque of St. Sophia is splendid, but no Christian is allowed to enter its precincts; the Turks themselves enter barefoot.'[20]

Caroline was unable to stay long in Constantinople on account of the plague, though Flora Fraser reports that she 'enjoyed a frenzied bout of shopping,' which, it seems, got charged to the British Embassy, including 'four dresses of embroidered gold brocade, and other gold clothes.'[21] Then, after stopping for a while on the other side of the Bosphorus, she headed back to Mytilene and Ephesus.

Now she was approaching what was intended to be the climax of the long voyage, her tour of the Holy Land. When she disembarked at Acre, one other English lady was far from welcoming: the slightly mad Lady Hester Stanhope, who had once been in Caroline's service and described her as a 'downright whore,'[22] rushed off to Antioch, where she pretended to have business with the British consul.[23] Caroline, planning her triumphal entry into Jerusalem, was above such petty irritations. Demont's Journal succeeds in turning this solemn occasion into a scene which, reproduced repeatedly in paintings and drawings, is irresistibly comic:

> At three o'clock in the same afternoon we broke up our tents, and the same evening, at nine o'clock, reached Jerusalem. At our entry, the people assembled in crowds to see the Princess of Wales who rode upon an ass. This circumstance recalled to me strongly the Day of Palms (Palm Sunday), on

---

[19] Louise Demont, *op. cit.*, 33–4.
[20] Louise Demont, *op. cit.*, 35.
[21] Flora Fraser, *op. cit.*, 286–7.
[22] Christopher Hibbert, *George III: A Personal History* (London, Viking, 1998), 355.
[23] Flora Fraser, *op. cit.*, 286–7.

which our Saviour made, in the same manner, his entry into Jerusalem. I imagined I beheld him, and inwardly made comparisons: for assuredly, if any one can in any way resemble our great Saviour, it is this excellent Princess. She is, like him, charitable, mild, and beneficent to all; she has suffered much, and always supports her misfortunes with great patience and resignation; and, like him, she has not deserved them.[24]

From then on Caroline was busy visiting the sacred sites like the chapel of St Helena, of whom Demont, not entirely at home with English history, gives this deliciously garbled account:

We began with the church, which was built by St. Helena. This virtuous Queen of England followed her husband to the crusades, and founded, it is said, five hundred churches, and as many hospitals. A more beneficent Queen it is impossible to imagine. She died in endeavouring to save the life of her husband, who had been wounded in the arm by an envenomed arrow; she extracted the poison by sucking the wound, and thus saved him, but was herself the victim of her excessive tenderness. Her husband caused her body to be transported to England, and on each spot where the vehicle which bore it rested, he erected a cross. The crosses still remain. The Queen was classed among the saints.[25]

However worthy her intentions, it is always difficult to take Caroline quite seriously: even her most loyal friends, like Gell and Charlotte Bury, made fun of her in their correspondence.

The visit to Jerusalem was the last triumph of Caroline's journey. She lived in Italy until George III died in 1820, when she insisted on returning to London as Queen. George IV promptly forced her to face another inconclusive 'trial' in the House of Lords, and then refused her admission to Westminster Abbey for what by rights should have been her coronation. A few months later she died in Brandenburgh House, the Hammersmith home of Elizabeth Craven, loaned no doubt thanks to Keppel. He and Gell remained her faithful chamberlains throughout the trial, before returning to the Margravine in Naples, where in the fullness of time they were all three buried in the same tomb.

---

[24] Louise Demont, *op. cit.*, 41–2.
[25] *Ibid.* 43–4.

Bibliography

Aspinall, Arthur, *The Letters of King George IV, 1812–1830*, 3 vols (Cambridge, Cambridge University Press, 1938).

Broadley, A. M. & Melville, Lewis (eds), *The Beautiful Lady Craven. The original memoirs of Elizabeth Baroness Craven afterwards Margravine of Anspach ... 1750–1828* (London, John Lane, 1914) Caroline, Princess, letter to Sir William Gell (21 April 1816), Derbyshire Record Office, D3287.

Craven, Elizabeth, *A Journey through the Crimea to Constantinople. In a series of letters from the right honourable Elizabeth Lady Craven to His Serene Highness the Margrave of Brandebourg, Anspach, and Bareith. Written in the year MDCCLXXXVI* (London, 1789).

Craven, Elizabeth, *Letters from the Right Honourable Lady Craven to his Serene Highness the Margrave of Anspach, during her travels through France, Germany, and Russia in 1785 and 1786* (London, 1814) [Note: this is the second edition of the above, but greatly enlarged and edited.].

Demont, Louise, *Voyages and Travels of Her Majesty, Caroline Queen of Great Britain..etc*, (London, 1821).

Dictionary of National Biography, 'Anspach, Elizabeth, Margravine'.

Fraser, Flora, *The Unruly Queen: the Life of Queen Caroline* (London, Macmillan, 1996).

Hibbert, Christopher, *George III: A Personal History* (London, Viking, 1998).

Wilson, Frances, *The Courtesan's Revenge* (London, Faber, 2003).

4. Travels in the Slavonic Provinces of Turkey-in-Europe: Miss Muir Mackenzie and Miss Irby

Dorothy Anderson

Many Victorian ladies who travelled and wrote about their travels are still remembered, admired for their fortitude, zeal and industry. It is surprising, therefore, that two women, Georgina Muir Mackenzie and Adeline Paulina Irby, held in high regard during their lives, have been neglected, almost forgotten. They were exceptional, intrepid travellers and so much more – scholars, educationalists, relief workers and, according to Florence Nightingale, political agitators.[1]

Looking back at their lives, it would seem that the impetus for all that they undertook and achieved as travellers, and for the dedication and enthusiasm with which they pursued their subsequent undertakings, originated from one incident, unpleasant, frightening, which they suffered during a stay at a small spa in the Carpathian mountains in 1859. It gave a purpose to their lives, a career and a mission.

To appreciate these changes is to reflect on their background, to consider the demands and restrictions of the society into which they were born. Both were ladies of quality and independence, and in 1859 neither had reached her thirtieth year. Georgina Muir Mackenzie was the eldest daughter of Sir John Muir Mackenzie of Delvine, Perthshire. Paulina Irby was the youngest daughter of the second son of Lord Boston. There was a tendency to consumption in the Muir Mackenzie family and Georgina was delicate. Paulina was more robust, in

---

[1] See Dorothy Anderson, *Miss Irby and Her Friends* (London, Hutchinson, 1966).

Adeline Paulina Irby: in old age, frontispiece from the Sarajevo journal, Prosvjeta, October 1st, 1911, death, funeral (also used in ODNB article).

temperament as well as health. They were well educated, interested in literature and antiquities, not politically active.

They set out on their travels in 1858, making an extended tour of Germany and the Austrian Empire, travelling leisurely, with visits to spas, to 'benefit [Georgina's] delicate health by change of air and scene'. In the summer of 1859 they decided to travel from Vienna to Cracow, not by train, but directly and slowly across the Carpathian mountains. They went alone, without a maid, journeying in hay carts, stopping often, visiting picturesque waterfalls and ruins, talking with influential people (they were fluent German speakers) about history, scenery, antiquities. They disregarded warnings of danger, were confident in their abilities to cope with awkward situations, and they had faith in their British passports. A month later they were back in Vienna, having found the journey 'easy in its transit and rich in its rewards'.

This was not quite accurate: their mode of travel – hay carts and such like – may have been pleasant and 'easy in transit', but they had suffered a particular indignity. At the hotel at the small spa of Schmocks, they had been arrested as spies and accused of 'Panslavism'. The incident had been unpleasant, woken early, 4 a.m., by gendarmes invading their hotel room, forced to dress with the men at their open door, taken under armed escort to police headquarters, themselves and their luggage searched and threatened with detention. Finally they were dismissed, allowed to return to their hotel and leave the town, but there was further police interference during the remainder of their journey. On their return to Vienna they registered a serious complaint with the British ambassador. They also prepared for publication their account of the incident.[2]

In the Public Record Office are the Foreign Office documents [FO 7/575], including the original letter from the ladies, the ambassador's complaint to the Austrian Ministry of Police on their behalf and the minister's explanation and apology. Their joint letter, four foolscap pages, written in alternate paragraphs, the angular disciplined hand of Georgina contrasting with Paulina's untidy scrawl, gives a full account of their arrest and of the accusations by gendarmes and officials, that they were suspected of 'Panslavism'. The minister, in his apology, justified the officials' actions, claiming that the two women 'had rendered themselves liable to be charged with imprudence by their demeanour, their intercourse with other persons, and the expressions used by them …'

The two women, however, saw no reason to apologise for their conduct. The incident proved not a deterrent, but rather the motivation for further travel, research and investigation. At the time of their arrest, they had been ignorant of the term 'Panslavism'. They now set themselves the task of learning about the Slavonic people, not those in the countries of the Austrian Empire but the more remote South Slavs, those living within the Ottoman Empire. For the next three years they travelled back and forth across the Balkans (the provinces of Turkey-in-Europe), to Constantinople, Salonica, Sophia, Belgrade, Sarajevo, Ragusa, Trieste, Agram, Northern Albania, the Ionian Islands.

Five journeys they made, travelling in four-wheeled carts, covered wagons without springs, litters slung between horses, and more comfortably by horseback. Always they were accompanied by dragomans and guards, sometimes three, sometimes twenty. To improve their investigations, they learnt Serbo-Croat and some Bulgarian. Wherever they stayed, they inquired into, and examined, the conditions of Christian Slavs under the Turks, made copious

---

[2] See footnote 4 below; quotations are from their book.

notes and accumulated evidence of Turkish misrule. They also made comparisons with 'free' Serbia (that principality had been self governing since 1817)
where there was no need for guards, there were schools and passable roads.

A map of the Balkans shows the places they visited and the distances they
travelled, but does not reveal the particular geographical features of the region
and consequent physical obstacles they faced: the mountains of northern Greece,
Albania, Bulgaria, Montenegro, the difficult passes, turbulent rivers, swamps,
the roads which were little more than tracks. A brief description of one incident
in their travels, as they told it, gives an indication of their difficulties, and of
their fortitude and energy in combating them.[3]

It happened early in their journey north from Salonica towards Vodena and
Monastir. There were problems with the dragomans and demands for payment
in advance, but they stayed firm: 'we required obedience and would listen to no
terms'. Their insistence won through and they finally set out, but so late that
they rode in the full heat of the day. At Vodena they stayed in comfort in the
home of a Swiss merchant, but 'sitting in the garden in the cool of the evening
caught the fever'. They travelled on and were forced to stay in a miserable *khan*
[inn], 'in a tiny room, with mud walls and floor, no glass in windows, and some
difficulty in fastening the door'. In the morning they were too ill to continue: '…
we found our only course was to lie still, drink hot tea, and imbibe medicine so
as to tide over the fever fit, and be able to take quinine…' They were no better
the next day and 'faced up to the fear of dying in reality, and dying in this
detestable *khan*.' They were rescued by the British consul at Monastir, and
though their strength 'was not sufficiently re-established to allow any lengthened
expedition', they visited the schools, distributing a collection of books (mostly
spelling books). They made plans for the next stages of their journey, this time,
given their weaken state, by carriage, 'a sort of covered wagon drawn by two
stout horses… assisted by oxen'. They carried on, the problems of transport,
payment of guards, wagons and horses ever with them.

Their resolution and stubbornness won through, fortified by their certainty
that nothing really disastrous would happen to them because they were British.
Their convictions were reinforced with each stay in a small town, every tale they
heard of another Turkish atrocity, every question they asked about the position
of women and schools for girls.

Their persistence was matched by a certain insensitivity. They were privileged
travellers through Turkish territory, with a special passport, a *firman*, and with
accompanying Turkish guards and accepting in towns the hospitality of Turkish
officials. They then demanded that they talk with Christian subjects, visit
Christian schools, inquire into the state of Christian women. They did not take
into consideration the possible aftermath of their questions on those Christian

---

[3] See footnote 6 below, Chapter 6, 'From Salonica to Monastir', 56–8.

subjects after they had moved on. Their conviction was complete, they had became ardent champions of the South Slavs. They had also identified and determined on their own special mission: to improve the conditions of Christian Slav women through education.

They wrote of their experiences and their investigations. Their first book, entitled *Across the Carpathians,* was published anonymously in 1862, an account of their 1859 journey and the spy incident and written as though by one author, travelling with her 'aunt'. In among the descriptions of bad beds, fleas, waterfalls and picturesque peasants, are chapters on aspects of the complexities of the Austrian Empire and one on 'Panslavism' which reveal scholarship and a forceful pen. Indeed both women had contributed to the text, and were as different as authors in style, interests and scholarship, as they were in personalities. (And the anonymity was conventional rather than serious, with a dedication to Lady Muir Mackenzie 'under whose roof these pages were written'.) There was further pretence of anonymity in a lengthy article, 'Christmas in Montenegro by I.M.', which appeared in an anthology of travel in 1862.[4]

For three years they travelled, but in the end delicate health, neglected in their enthusiasm, could not be ignored. However slowly they travelled, whatever precautions they took, they found themselves succumbing to the persisting evils of 'Danubian fever, indifferent food and lodging'. Finally, 'when health and strength failed us, there was nothing for it but to come home.'

This they did in 1864. At the meeting of the British Association in Bath, Miss Muir Mackenzie, the only woman speaker, contributed a paper on travel in the South Slavonic countries of Austria and Turkey. Her paper in extended form was published in 1865, with a lengthy title and again anonymously.[5] At the British Association meeting in Birmingham in 1865, the two, the only women speakers, presented a paper on the characteristics of the Slavonic races.

The extent of their travels and knowledge of the Balkan countries was revealed in 1867 with the publication of their major work, *Travels in the Slavonic provinces of Turkey-in-Europe*, a substantial volume of 688 pages, with maps, appendices, illustrations, glossary and footnotes – evidence of much research. The names of the two authors, with initials, appear on the title-page but within the text there is no identification of either woman: 'our gloves', 'we asked', 'the horse of one of us bolted'. But after the contents pages, there is a note: 'The greater portion of the text is contributed by the writer whose name stands first

---

[4] [G. Muir Mackenzie and A. P. Irby], *Across the Carpathians.* In Francis Galton, ed., *Vacation tourists and notes of travel in 1861* (London, Macmillan, 1862) Chapter 11, 357–418.

[5] Humphry Sandwith (ed.), *Notes on the South Slavonic countries in Austria and Turkey in Europe, containing historical and political information added to the substance of a paper read at the British Association at Bath, 1864* (Edinburgh, Blackwood, 1865).

on the title-page.'[6] Georgina was acknowledged as the scholar, writing with authority, enthusiastic yet detached, committed yet critical.

The two had also been active in looking for ways to advance their own special mission, to provide education for Christian Slav girls. Their first step, in 1865, was to set up in London the 'Association for the Promotion of Education among the Slavonic Children of Bosnia and Herzegovina', with its particular objective the establishment of a school. This was to be in Sarajevo, the very heart of Bosnia, a city almost medieval, oriental, secretive. Georgina began correspondence with the British consul in Sarajevo about their plans.

The Association attracted little attention and there were increasing difficulties about the practicality of its objective. Georgina's health was failing and she could no longer contemplate lengthy visits and responsibilities abroad. Paulina had found a new enthusiasm: she had met Florence Nightingale and had become one of Miss Nightingale's circle of devoted friends. A solution was found whereby the funds collected were entrusted to the Protestant deaconesses at the Kaiserswerth Institution in Germany (Paulina had had some training there and earlier Miss Nightingale). Land was bought, a school house built and the school opened in Sarajevo in 1869.

This could well have been the end of their endeavours, for Georgina and Paulina had come to the parting of ways. Georgina had travelled to Corfu, in search of improved health and to renew a friendship made when they had visited the Ionian Islands and had stayed with Sir Charles Sebright, now British consul in Corfu. In 1871 Georgina and Sir Charles were married. He was much older than her, a widower of dignity and charm, with a Scottish background like herself, and he had held official appointments in the Ionian Islands since 1842 (when the Islands were a British protectorate). When the Islands became Greek in 1864, he had stayed on as British consul, with a reputation for ability and honesty. It was perhaps a surprising decision for Georgina but she had found a haven, sympathetic care, comfort and tranquillity for the little time that remained. She died three years later and was buried in Corfu. She had not forgotten the South Slavs and in her will she set up a trust fund to provide money to be paid annually to:

> A Christian youth and a Christian woman of Serbian race and language, who shall best qualify themselves for teaching the poorer classes in the most ignorant parts of their own country.[7]

The school under the deaconesses did not prosper. There was dislike of their uniforms and suspicion of their religious aims. In 1871 they withdrew, and Paulina accepted the challenge to take on the direction of the school herself (and in so doing may well have had Miss Nightingale's encouragement). In Sarajevo

---

[6] G. Muir Mackenzie and A. P. Irby, *Travels in the Slavonic provinces of Turkey-in-Europe: the Turks, the Greeks, and the Slavons* (London, Bell & Daldy, 1867).

[7] Anderson, *op.cit.*, 71.

she faced considerable problems. It was difficult to persuade Bosnians that daughters were worthy of education, even more difficult to convince them that the aim of the school was education and that all girls, Orthodox, Catholic and even Muslim, would be welcome.

Her position became more comfortable when a new companion, Priscilla Johnston, joined her in 1872. Priscilla had a family connection with Paulina and a family tradition to follow. She was the granddaughter of Sir Thomas Fowell Buxton, the anti-slavery campaigner, and the great-niece of Elizabeth Fry. Together Paulina and Priscilla succeeded in establishing the school securely, with their own routine of responsibilities, spending most of the year in Sarajevo, returning to England for a summer vacation, Paulina with Miss Nightingale, Priscilla with her family.

This pattern was broken when revolt against Turkish rule erupted in Bosnia in August 1875. In Sarajevo there was something akin to panic, and Paulina and Priscilla acted promptly, taking their five best pupils to a girls' school in Prague. As they fled Sarajevo, they saw the first evidence of the uprisings, refugees crowding over the river Sava to seek the safety of Austrian soil. It gave them the impetus for a new endeavour, more challenging and public: they would return to the frontier to bring aid to the refugees and establish schools for the refugee children.

Back in England they set about gathering funds for their new purpose. An appeal letter for the 'Bosnian and Herzegovinian Fugitives' Orphan Relief Fund' (a clumsy and confusing title) was published in *The Times*, November 1875, setting out the aims of the Fund, with a list of distinguished friends and supporters. At the end of the year they returned to Croatia and through the winter months worked along the frontier, in snow, mud, smallpox and typhus, distributing corn and blankets. By the summer, when they returned to England, they had also established eight schools where over four hundred refugee children were fed, clothed, housed and taught.

In England they were caught up in the emotional fever of the Bulgarian atrocities agitation. The reporter from the *Daily News* had described in detail scenes he had witnessed in Bulgaria: impaled bodies hanging like scarecrows on river banks featured largely. Other accounts, no less sensational, appeared in other papers. Throughout the country hundreds of meetings were being held and thousands of pounds were pouring in to help the suffering Christians under Turkish rule. There were many relief funds, with names and aims differing only slightly, some of dubious motivation and responsibility, but there was no hesitation among the British public, just an overwhelming response that extended on into the next year.[8]

---

[8] See R. T. Shannon, *Gladstone and the Bulgarian Agitation 1876* (London, Nelson, 1963). See Dorothy Anderson, *The Balkan Volunteers* (London, Hutchinson, 1968) for an account of the work of the various relief funds.

10 Ovington Gardens, London—sorting and packing clothes
for the destitute in the Turkish provinces

10 Ovington Gardens, London – sorting and packing clothes for the destitute in the Turkish provinces, Illustrated London News, *October 7th, 1876.*

For Paulina and Priscilla the situation was bewildering – and infuriating. Little notice had been taken of the Bosnian uprisings, but now because of descriptions of atrocities in Bulgaria, money flowed. A more balanced view, more accurate accounts of conditions throughout the Ottoman Empire were required and they were fortunate that they had many supporters well established in high places and eloquent with pen and voice. There were the Irby and Johnston family connections, which included bankers, MPs, humanitarians, Liberals, and there was the influential circle around Miss Nightingale. It was their relief fund that featured as the front cover of the *Illustrated London News,* October 7th, 1876.

Even more effective in publicising their Fund was Paulina's visit to Mr

Gladstone, who found her outspoken indictment of Turkish rule admirable. He lectured on conditions in the Ottoman Empire, making use of their book, referred to it favourably in the House of Commons and contributed a preface to its second edition which Paulina was preparing early in 1877. Paulina wrote in appreciation to Mr Gladstone on April 10th, adding that she had sent it to Miss Nightingale who had found that 'it had done her good to read it.'[9]

On July 16th there was a well-attended public meeting in support of the Fund at which Mr Gladstone spoke at length in praise of Miss Irby and Miss Johnston. *The Times* of July 17th provided a two-page account of the meeting, reporting Mr Gladstone's speech at length, with shorter extracts from those of the other distinguished gentlemen present.

At the end of 1876 Paulina and Priscilla resumed their work, making their headquarters in the small town of Knin in Dalmatia. A letter from Priscilla on January 16th, 1877 gave an emotional description of the situation they faced and their consequent feeling of inadequacy:

> We had about 3,000 Bosnians about us, though we could only distribute linen enough for one shirt to each child. Over 600 received it, together with sewing thread, and a large hard biscuit of black bread... It seemed to us impossible that human beings could be reduced to the objects before us. The sunken glassy eyes, the protruding bones scarcely covered, and the deathly colour of most of them ...

Her letter with a report from Paulina, and an appeal for more funds, was published in one of the campaigning pamphlets of the Eastern Question Association.[10] They now had another helper, skilful with words and enthusiastic in his reporting, the young Arthur Evans (later the archaeologist of Knossos), writing in the *Manchester Guardian*. His descriptions of refugees dependent upon the 'relief trains' of Miss Irby and Miss Johnston ensured that questions were asked in the House of Commons with Liberal MPs quoting from their letters.

Paulina had left the business affairs of the Fund in the hands of Miss Nightingale but in Miss Nightingale's eyes Paulina lacked method, sometimes common sense and had difficulty in distinguishing between the 'orphans' that featured in the Fund's title and refugee children with mothers. Miss Nightingale was critical and exasperated and her written comments at the bottom of Paulina's letters were cruel: 'If only she would give us some facts instead of writing like a German newspaper; If only she would make up her mind whether she is a political agitator or a reliever of distress; How many lies I have told!' But she

---

[9] 2nd ed. With a preface by the Rt. Hon. W. E. Gladstone. 2 vols. (London, Daldy & Ibister, 1877). [Vol.1 includes the preface, additional chapters by A. P. Irby, followed by the text of the 1867 edition].

[10] M. G. Fawcett, *The martyrs of Turkish misrule. With a supplement by Miss Irby*. (Pamphlet No.5) (London, Eastern Question Association 1877) 19–24.

ensured that the name of the Fund was now more accurate: 'Fugitives and Orphans'.

The revolt in Bosnia simmered on into 1878, the number of refugees swelled and still Paulina and Priscilla distributed food, cared for orphans and maintained schools (at one time twenty one schools with over twelve hundred children). Miss Nightingale, becoming more appreciative of her friend's work, did as much as she could to help: revising appeals, rewriting reports and trying to curb Paulina's involvement in politics.

But Paulina continued to be pro-Slav and violently anti-Turk, and had no wish to be discreet. It was not surprising when, after the Treaty of Berlin, June, 1878, Bosnia and Herzegovina were placed under Austrian jurisdiction, that the Austrian authorities were reluctant to allow Miss Irby and Miss Johnston to return to Sarajevo. It was not until her influential friends had interceded that permission was given. There was a great welcome in Sarajevo and their school prospered.

As the necessary continuation of their work they also maintained an orphanage. Priscilla, writing on August 17th, 1880, described the year since their return to Sarajevo, of sixty-six orphan boys and girls living in three houses, of their training, schooling, and of how many of the older boys had learnt trades and were now working. Her letter was included in another fund appeal written by Margaret Evans (Arthur Evans' wife) in *The Monthly Packet*, in which she included a useful paragraph, specifying the anticipated costs for the current year at £800 'of which half has been promised by the directresses themselves.'[11] Two years later, after a three-month visit to Sarajevo, she wrote about their school, with descriptions of its site, the daily schedule, the pupils (about thirty). Her article, entitled 'The English school in Sarajevo', also included an appeal for funds to help 'Miss Irby and Miss Johnston in this excellent work of theirs, for the expenses of feeding and clothing so many children are necessarily great.'[12]

During the next few years Paulina's routine changed as the school and Sarajevo became her permanent home. Her political interests and her pro-Slav attachments had strengthened and she focused on Serbia and Serbians. The original aim of the Association – 'education for Slavonic children' – was ignored. She had become the staunch advocate of the greater Serbia, looking towards the creation of a South Slav state that would incorporate Bosnia, Herzegovina, Croatia, Serbia and Dalmatia. Within the school, Austrian edicts were largely ignored and pupils were encouraged to be Orthodox in their religion, Serb in their speech and customs.

---

[11] Margaret Evans, 'Bosnian refugees fund', *The Monthly Packet*, Vol. 30, November 1880, 499–500.

[12] Margaret Evans, 'The English school in Sarajevo', *The Monthly Packet*, Vol. 32, February 1882, 198–200.

In 1885 Priscilla returned to England and to her family. There are no records of why she left the school; probably she was increasingly ill at ease with Paulina's political Serbian obsession; or perhaps she felt she had followed the family tradition for long enough. She went to live with her sister near Carlisle, became 'Aunt Pris' to all, mildly eccentric in her attentions to animals. She died in 1912, with that early active period of her life 'in the Balkans' forgotten by her family. One relic was found: a 'Bosnian boy's costume', preserved in an attic, its source and history unknown.

Paulina stayed on in Sarajevo until her death in 1911. Her last account of the school was presented at an international conference on education in Chicago, 1893 (but it is very doubtful that she was there).[13] The school survived and she continued as its directress and benefactor. But increasingly her interests and energies were concentrated on matters political. In the inner circles of conspiracy that enveloped Bosnia in the early twentieth century, Miss Irby, the English lady, old, nearly blind and immobile, had her place as a Serb patriot. At her funeral mourners came from all over Bosnia and from the Kingdom of Serbia. The issue of the Sarajevo journal, *Prosvjeta*, October 1911, presented as its frontispiece a portrait of Miss Irby in old age.[14]

In 1934 celebrations in commemoration of the centenary of her birth (she was actually born in 1831) were held in Sarajevo and throughout Yugoslavia, the South Slav state created in 1918, the fulfilment of her dream. In the years following, on June 28th, the anniversary of the day when the student, Gavrilo Princip, fired the shot that precipitated the First World War, a ceremony was held in the Orthodox Church at the plaque that commemorated the conspirators; and then those assembled moved from the church to the cemetery, and a prayer was said before the grave of Paulina Irby.[15] Sarajevo believed that she had been as much a Serbian patriot as Gavrilo Princip.

---

[13] A. P. Irby, 'English orphanage and training school on Bosnia, 1869–1892', *Proceedings of the International Congress of Education, Chicago, 1893* (New York, National Educational Association, 1895), 900–3.

[14] See also: Arthur J. Evans, 'The late Miss Irby: a tribute', *The Contemporary Review*, December, 1911, 844–6.

[15] She was buried in the Protestant cemetery, and when that was destroyed in town planning operations, was re-buried in the Orthodox church cemetery.

5. Three Travellers in Nineteenth Century Egypt: Sarah Belzoni, Amelia Edwards and Margaret Benson

Megan Price

I made the acquaintance of these three women through my own growing interest in Egypt and Egyptology. The first, Sarah Belzoni, I discovered through studying the exploits of her husband Gianbattista Belzoni. At the Temple of Ramses II at Abu Simbel a brief description of his unorthodox excavation activities was given by the tour guide as the carving of his name on the entrance was pointed out to me. His role in the history of Egyptology is only briefly acknowledged in references to the Egyptian exhibits in the British Museum which he had collected. The work of Margaret Benson at the Temple of Mut at Karnak was brought to my attention during my own visit to the temple complex, carrying the Baedeker guidebook for 1908, which mentioned the work on the Temple of Mut by Miss Benson, an English lady 'who had cleaned it of rubbish'.[1] Finally, following my interest in Sarah Belzoni and Margaret Benson, I decided to read about the experiences of Amelia Edwards who had, through serendipity, also travelled in Egypt and recorded her observations. I wanted to know more about women travellers and their responses to Egypt.

From their early beginnings, humans have always been intrigued by the attraction of the other. In Palaeolithic times the search for food and shelter was paramount. By the time people settled, built shelters and created elaborate permanent buildings out of stone, brick or baked mud, the urge to explore and travel became more systemised and regular. The setting up of trade networks for exchanging goods and exploring and creating new settlements was

---

[1] Baedecker, 1908, 276.

established well before the period of Dynastic Egypt in the third millennium BC. The obligation, need, urge, wish or whim to travel is a very human attribute and whether for employment or pleasure much of our time can be and is spent 'on the move', looking for something new, an opportunity, an opening.

I examine this phenomenon as it was experienced by three particular women travellers, Sarah Belzoni, Amelia Edwards and Margaret Benson, all from very different English backgrounds who, by chance, arrived in Egypt during the nineteenth century. Before describing their experiences, I will give a brief description of the rediscovery of ancient Egypt by Europeans.

The early part of the nineteenth century was not only the time of the birth of Egyptology following Napoleon's expedition in 1798, but also of the wholesale and indiscriminate plundering of many of the tombs and monuments in the name of culture and historical investigation – or looting and piracy. This was carried out and recorded by and large by gentlemen travellers – British, Italian and French; some honest, some not so honest; some as foreign consuls for their countries with *carte blanche* to obtain Egyptian antiquities. Others employed agents, such as Belzoni, to obtain these objects 'to order'. This nineteenth century pillaging was in fact nothing new; the ancient Egyptians themselves had also been systematic tomb-looters, as had the Roman emperors – Hadrian and Diocletian for instance. As an academic and scientific discipline concerned with recording rather than removing antiquities, Egyptian archaeology did not exist until the late nineteenth century.

Within this background, I would like to establish my women travellers. The first, Sarah Belzoni (1783–1870), was the courageous and independent-minded wife of the 'greatest tomb robber of all' – Gianbattista Belzoni, (1778–1825). The couple travelled to Egypt, where Belzoni was hoping to find employment, and remained there from 1815 to 1819. The second woman traveller is Amelia Edwards, who, after deciding by chance to sail to Egypt to escape the bad weather during a holiday in the Mediterranean, made it her life's work to write about and protect Egypt's ancient treasures and enlighten the general public to their importance. The third travelling woman, again originally *en vacance* in the 1890s, 'almost stumbled' on the Temple of Mut, an unexcavated temple at Karnak and immediately began to organise and finance her own archaeological dig there for two seasons.

Sarah Belzoni (née Banne 1783–1870)

Unlike many travellers to Europe and Egypt in the early nineteenth century who wrote about their experiences, Sarah appears to have been from a lower middle or working class background. All that is known of her early life is that she was born in Bristol in 1783; there is no evidence of letters of recommendation, no connections, no family background or social network. Her *Trifling Account* included at the end of Gianbattista's grand *Narrative* shows that she had received some form of education. This is demonstrated by her sharp turns of phrase and observations on her experiences. In the *Account* and her later writing activities, there appears the voice of an individual with an independent mind, though unfortunately not with the benefit of independent means. It is probable that she was raised in a Christian environment. Her interest in visiting the Holy Land and references in her text to 'Christian and moral attitudes' suggest a well-informed Christian background. Certainly, like the biblical Naomi, Sarah followed Belzoni into Egypt believing that 'whither thou goest, I will go.'

It is likely that the couple met in London while Belzoni was earning his living as a strong man in Sadler's Wells Theatre.[2] He had left Padua, where he was born in 1778, and travelled in France and Holland with his brother in order to look for employment. In Rome he had studied hydraulics, a trade that was to stand him in good stead for future ventures into theatrical spectaculars. He eventually arrived in London where he became a familiar figure, travelling from fair to fair, performing acts of strength as 'The Great Belzoni'. He met Sarah during eight years in Britain and presumably they married; although no certificate of marriage or entry has yet come to light, passport documents exist, with Sarah described as his wife, issued by the Governor of Malta on May 9th 1815. It is possible that Belzoni was in Ireland in 1807 and 1812 and certainly their faithful servant James Curtin was Irish; perhaps Sarah was too. In February 1814 Belzoni went to Oxford where he performed at the Blue Boar Inn, St Aldate's to a large undergraduate audience.[3]

In 1815, at the age of thirty-two, Sarah sailed with Belzoni via Malta to Alexandria. Here she experienced her first taste of Egypt, in quarantine from the plague. They were confined for three or four days and at once were taken ill, not with plague themselves, but with stomach cramps, which they had to conceal from the authorities in case they became plague suspects. In Cairo the Belzonis were provided with a bare ramshackle house; Sarah called this her drawing room. Fortunately at that time people were used to travelling 'heavy': Sarah had sheets, mattresses, plates, knives and forks, which they had used on the boat from England. Sarah was probably resourceful and used to the unexpected; for example she dealt calmly with a knife wound Belzoni received from a Turkish soldier in the street and remained unperturbed by the performance of professional belly dancers, the *ghawazi*, at their neighbour's wedding.

The Belzonis had travelled to Egypt in hopes of promised employment but disaster struck the first attempt: Belzoni had constructed a hydraulic machine to carry the water from the Nile but it appeared to be unworkable [– or perhaps it failed when being used by Egyptian workers]. Following an introduction by the Swiss explorer Burckhardt, Belzoni obtained a commission from Henry Salt,

---

[2] *Playbill,* May 9th 1803.
[3] Notes and Queries, 1864, 44.

British consul-general in Egypt, to remove the head of Memnon from a temple site at Thebes about ten days' sail south from Cairo. By July 1816, with great effort and ingenuity he had succeeded in removing this head, using a team of three hundred local workers, and had it transported it overland to a boat on the Nile, from where it was to be taken by boat to England. It can now be seen in the Egypt galleries of the British Museum, though Belzoni's contribution to its acquisition is unacknowledged.

Sarah and Gianbattista then sailed on further up the Nile towards Aswan and the first Cataract. On 27th August they reached Philae and, after fighting off a group of natives who attempted to board their ship, sailed on to Abu Simbel where news had come through of an immense temple with four colossal statues at the entrance. After narrowly escaping shipwreck below the Cataract, Belzoni arranged to begin clearing the sand from the Temple of Rameses II at Abu Simbel, leaving Sarah on board the boat, moored a little way off. One morning two labourers attempted to board the boat but Sarah with presence of mind waved a pistol at them. By this time she had learned the art of survival.

There are other occasions when Sarah was left alone, for instance with an Egyptian family in Luxor for six weeks and in June 1817, more astonishingly, she camped with only James Curtin, a servant boy, in what she termed the 'Temple of Osiris' on the island of Philae where the temperature was 140°F in the shade.[4] Sarah and Curtin were left with a large quantity of luggage and a pair of pistols. Belzoni and the rest of his party had sailed to Abu Simbel to visit 'the noblest monument of antiquity that is to be found on the banks of the Nile' but they could not afford a place for Sarah on board. She remained at Philae for two months, only seeing local women who came across to the island to view this curiosity and with whom she traded beads and small mirrors in exchange for eggs and arrows and little 'anticas'.

Possibly having had these enforced tastes of independence, in 1818 Sarah decided to visit the Holy Land with Curtin and another Italian traveller, Giovanni Finati. In Jerusalem Sarah visited the Mosque of Omar and the Dome of the Rock dressed as a Muslim merchant. The Mosque was prohibited to infidels and women, but must have appeared a great challenge to Sarah. She made her way back to Cairo to meet Belzoni who had just returned from the Red Sea.

They left Thebes in Upper Egypt for the last time in January 1818, taking an assorted cargo consisting of an obelisk, a sarcophagus, mummies and moulds. This time Sarah was left at Rosetta with her pet chameleons whilst Belzoni set off again for the Fayyum to the west of the Nile.[5]

The Belzonis' book describing their endeavours in Egypt, *Narrative of the Operations and Recent Discoveries*, was first published in 1820 and ran into many

---

[4] 'Sarah's 'Trifling Account', in Belzoni, *Narrative,* 1820, 452.
[5] *Ibid.,* 371.

editions. Sarah's own account of her travels and impressions was included at the back as 'A Trifling Account'; it adds much colour and individuality. Sarah's contribution consists of forty pages describing her own experiences. What makes them unique is her frankness of observation: 'Having heard so much of Turks and Arabs, I took the opportunity while in Egypt to observe the manners of the women in that country.'[6] Whenever 'Mr B' went off to look for antiquities, Sarah went to meet women from the villages. In the preface to the *Narrative* Belzoni declares it to be his own work, but if it is compared with his letters in the Banks archive in Dorchester Record Office his book displays a great difference in style, syntax, punctuation and spelling. Possibly Sarah Belzoni had more of a hand in it than just her own 'trifling account'.

Throughout his activities in the East, Belzoni and Sarah were constantly held back by being either foreign or from the 'wrong' class. In Egypt, they suffered to some extent the same treatment as the indigenous population. They were given tasks to perform by Banks and Salt and were treated, paid and rewarded as servants.

On their return to England in 1821 the Belzonis set up an exhibition at the Egyptian Hall, Piccadilly. It consisted of two full-scale reproductions of chambers from the Tomb of Seti 1, a fifty-foot model and their collection of scarabs, *ushabtis* and two mummies.

Their last journey together was in 1823 to Morocco; from there Belzoni travelled on to Timbuktu possibly trying to trace the source of the Niger but died on December 3rd of dysentery. It is believed that he was buried under a tree on the roadside. An inscription bearing his name and the date of his death 3rd December 1823, was commissioned by the ship's carpenter, it read: 'G. Belzoni Esq. who was attacked by dysentery at Benin on his way to Houssa and Timbuctu'. It was requested that every European visiting the spot should clear the ground and repair the fence around the grave. By 1862, when the traveller Sir Richard Burton went to visit it, no trace remained.

In his last letter to his friend and sponsor of the expedition, Samuel Briggs, Belzoni set out arrangements for his possessions: 'The next thing is what I feel most deep to my heart: console my poor Sarah: tell her I cannot write to her; she has been to me a most faithful and dutiful wife upwards of twenty years.' With his tender affection, he sent his amethyst ring.[7] After his death Sarah attempted to hold another exhibition but it was not a success, nor was the sale of a commemorative lithograph. It would appear that she was left in some poverty and she attempted to sell objects belonging to her husband. It was not until 1852 that she was granted a pension of £100 a year. She died in St Helier, Jersey, on January 12th 1870. There is no trace of her grave.[8]

---

[6] *Ibid.*, 441.
[7] Mayes 1959, 285.
[8] Personal communication 2002, Marco Zatterin.

Amelia Edwards 1831–1892

Amelia Edwards was raised in a middle-class household; she was educated by her mother who, ambitious for her only daughter, engaged private teachers for music and drawing. Amelia was considered talented enough for professional training in either music or art but in her early twenties she turned to writing. By the early 1860s her parents had died and she was left without financial support. Like many unmarried women of this time she became a companion to an elderly widow.[9]

In 1873 she was travelling in Europe with her own companion, Lucy Renshawe, in continual rain. An impulsive decision to sail to Egypt to avoid the climate was to change the course and purpose of Amelia's future; she noted, 'had anyone ventured to inquire in so many words what brought us to Egypt we should have replied "stress of weather".'[10] The impact of 'the other' struck immediately; she was impressed by the bazaars, the mosques and the people of modern Egypt, but as her attention was drawn to the immense antiquity of the Egypt of the past she became transformed. Combining her writing skill with her capacity for astute and observant research, in 1887 she wrote *A Thousand Miles up the Nile* in order to 'educate the modern visitor' as she explained in the preface.

Unlike the Belzonis' experiences in 1815 of travel in Egypt, Amelia Edwards had sufficient financial and personal means to hire her own private *dahabiyyah* to sail to Upper Egypt. The *Philae* was a hundred feet long with eighteen sleeping cabins, a dining room and a bathroom.[11] As she had the financial means to be in control she was able to organise her visits to the ancient monuments in the same chronological order in which they had been built. The statuary, the reliefs and the frescoes appealed to her trained artist's eye and she recorded them without the romantic or dramatic effects that had been employed for instance by David Roberts in the 1830s.

At Karnak she found the scale of the columns was too vast for her to comprehend and she could only 'look and be silent'. Her attention was attracted by the Temple of Mut which Margaret Benson was to excavate. Here Amelia Edwards noticed that 'battered and forlorn sat a weird company of green granite sphinxes and lion headed beasts.'[12] At Philae she recorded the pathos and remoteness of where Sarah Belzoni had camped for two months in 1816, putting into words 'the melancholy beauty' that Sarah may have felt but could not articulate.

At Abu Simbel Amelia Edwards organised her crew into the excavation and restoration of a small temple. Perhaps this event convinced her that something

---

[9] Rees, 1998, 23.
[10] Edwards, 1888, 2.
[11] *Ibid.,* 39.
[12] *Ibid.,* 148–54.

ought to be done to preserve the monuments of ancient Egypt before they were defaced or acquired for European museums.

Returning to England in 1874 Amelia Edwards devoted her services and finances to Egypt and Egyptian scholarship and became a practical and moral supporter of the work of William Flinders Petrie (1853–1942). Her initial attempts to go 'grubbing for treasure' were forgotten as she embarked on her new mission. In 1882 she helped to found the Egyptian Exploration Fund (later the Egypt Exploration Society) and, from 1889 and 1890, she toured America giving lectures and receiving official recognition of her work from many universities.

Amelia died in 1891 after catching cold at Millwall Docks while supervising the unloading of Petrie's cases of archaeological finds from Egypt. Her will contained a bequest endowing a Professorship of Egyptian Archaeology and Philology at University College London, in such a way that only Flinders Petrie would qualify for the position, which he was then to hold for the next forty years. Although Petrie was self-taught and had no formal schooling, he received many honorary degrees and was made the Edwards Professor of Egyptology in 1892 and held that position until 1933.

From her chance visit to Egypt to escape the rains of Europe Amelia Edwards had given Egyptology academic recognition as a professional discipline. She did not look for immortality but hoped that through *A Thousand Miles* she would be remembered, 'if I hope to be remembered at all.'[13]

Margaret Benson 1865–1916

In the preface to her book *The Temple of Mut in Asher*, 1899, Margaret Benson admits, 'Our first intention was not ambitious. We were desirous of clearing a picturesque site. We were frankly warned that we should make no discoveries; indeed if any had been anticipated it was unlikely that the clearance would have been entrusted to inexperienced direction. On January 1st 1895, we began the excavation.'

Margaret was a member of the Benson family, a Victorian collection of upper-class clerical and highly eccentric people. *The Temple of Mut,* written with Janet Gourlay as her assistant, describes the work they carried out over the three seasons they spent at Karnak in Upper Egypt. Like Amelia Edwards, Margaret Benson discovered both Egypt and the temple site by chance.

Margaret, known to the family as 'Maggie', was always regarded as being delicate She appeared to be happiest studying at Oxford in the 1880s at the newly-founded Lady Margaret Hall, where in 1886 she gained a first-class degree in Moral Philosophy. After leaving Oxford, the upper-class social conventions

---

[13] Rees, *op. cit.,* 101.

of the period meant that Maggie was not able to pursue any career and she soon 'retreated into ill-health'.[14]

In 1893 she joined her brother Fred who at the time was excavating for the British School at Athens. Fred was later better known as E. F. Benson, author of the satirical *Mapp and Lucia* novels. In Greece Maggie was able to enjoy mixing in an intellectual society.

In 1894 she was advised to travel to the warmer climate of Egypt as she was suffering from rheumatism and arthritis. At Luxor she wrote: 'the place grows on one extraordinarily. I don't feel as if I should have really had an idea of Egypt at all if I hadn't stayed here – the immensity of the whole thing is beginning to dawn – and the colour – oh my goodness! You get to see them more every day.'[15] She had obviously been as impressed as Amelia Edwards had been twenty years earlier; after a period of illness and depression, and the European climate, they had both been 'surprised by joy'.

By November 1894 Maggie had conceived the idea of asking permission to excavate the ruined Temple of Mut at Karnak, a site that covered approximately twenty-two acres and consisted of three major temples and a crescent-shaped lake. By 1894 the ruins 'could hardly claim even half an hour's study', Maggie wrote, but she was intrigued by an avenue of sphinxes which led to 'a small ruined temple, roofless and with walls broken down ... in front of which two colossal statues are pitched forward. It was a place to seize on the imagination.'[16] Like Sarah Belzoni and Amelia Edwards, Maggie experienced the sentiments felt by many eighteenth and nineteenth century travellers – 'the east was calling'.

By 1895, with the assistance of Edouard Naville, (1844–1926), one of the first excavators for Amelia Edwards' Egyptian Exploration Fund, Maggie gained permission to excavate, though she did remark caustically in a letter to her mother that she would not have been given this assistance if it had been thought that she would discover anything.

At the age of thirty and a semi-invalid, Maggie became the first woman to conduct and organise her own excavation in Egypt with her assistant Janet Gourlay. The companions continued to excavate until 1897 working for three seasons, each of about two months in length, with various family members and friends. Shortly after her work in Egypt ceased, Maggie suffered from increasing bouts of mental illness. By 1906 she was being treated for manic depression and in 1907 she was committed to a private sanitorium. She never recovered and died in 1916.

Margaret was a member of the Benson family who, on their own admission, were a highly eccentric collection of people. Although they wrote intensely

---

[14] Askwith, 1971, 179.
[15] Benson, A. C., 1917, 169.
[16] Benson and Gourlay, 1899, 8–9.

about and to each other, Maggie's brother E. F. Benson later destroyed all family correspondence which may have given any cause for scandal. The only correspondence which would have been considered socially acceptable remains in the 'Benson Deposit' at the Bodleian library. The few letters there reveal great unhappiness.

In *Maggie Benson, her life and letters* her other brother A. C. Benson presents a eulogy rather than a biography in which his sister is portrayed as fitting the Victorian social norm for a gentlewoman. There are few suggestions of Maggie's increasing mental and physical illness. Few letters remain which describe any specific events relating to the family dynamics, but there is an Ibsen-like quality about the family's dark references to Maggie's 'illness' in her adult life.[17] Even letters written home during Maggie's excavations seem to be more concerned with her health than accounts of her recent findings.

Experiences and Narrative

Sarah Belzoni, Margaret Benson and Amelia Edwards were writing about their experiences before the sociology of the position of women was considered. Although aware that they were women in a male European world and in an Arab world, they were aware of the imposed cultural limitations. There were however advantages as well as disadvantages. In the Near East Sarah Belzoni was able to travel incognito, dressed in women or men's clothing according to her own choice or circumstances. (But she always wore her 'stays' underneath, whether posing as Egyptian merchant or European female).

Sarah was also able to visit the womens' quarters of several Egyptian households. This was a subject which had caused much intrigue and speculation during the eighteenth and nineteenth centuries amongst European artists and writers. Possibly her lack of social standing allowed her more freedom than those of a higher class. It has been said that the lower classes and the aristocracy were able to flaunt convention more easily. Those between were shackled by their middle-class morality. Sarah did not appear to be constricted by her marriage but rather by her social and financial position. Amelia Edwards and Margaret Benson were unmarried but able to support themselves financially and conduct themselves with suitable decorum. The influential introductions and connections made possible by Maggie Benson's and Amelia Edwards' social backgrounds enabled them to obtain permission, rights and invitations to visit places that were not available to the Belzonis. Maggie, for example, found no trouble in obtaining permission to dig, from M. Naville, the director of the site.

In Maggie's seasons of excavation 1895–6, the Benson family entourage accompanied her. By then travelling had been made easier by Thomas Cook enterprises in Egypt which began in the 1860s and it was perceived as a family

---

[17] Askwith, 222.

holiday. Amelia Edwards was also in the fortunate financial position of being able to organise her own travelling arrangements and choose her companions. A middle-class imperiousness combined with a full purse enabled her to both secure the best and to command the speed, direction and content of her journey and devote her time to her writing, sketches and entertaining visitors. This is not to belittle her achievements, but to indicate what a determined female with independent means was in a position to accomplish. Both Amelia and Maggie were later approached by established Egyptologists to write for the general public on this growing subject of interest. Percy Newberry the Egyptologist suggested to Maggie that she could research a history of Egypt and the French Egyptologist Gaston Maspero wanted Amelia to translate some of his works.

The nineteenth century saw the beginnings of professional archaeology, at first with a small and select group. Economic independence would appear to be a vital factor in the early years of any individual's archaeological pursuit. Archaeology may have been viewed as a leisure pursuit but this is no reason to dismiss or deny the contribution these women made during the nineteenth century.

The success of these women should enable them to be viewed as archaeologists. They were able to note damage to monuments, criticise dishonesty and deal with personnel with flair and tact. Sarah Belzoni claimed 'fair play' for her husband's contribution to British Egyptological collections; Amelia Edwards wished to forestall the destruction being done to many monuments; and Margaret Benson found in her excavations at the Temple of Mut a chance to examine a site which had been dismissed or ignored by previous French excavations.

Women as writers: Sarah Belzoni, 'A Trifling Account'; Amelia Edwards, *A 1000 Miles up the Nile;* and Margaret Benson and Janet Gourlay, *The Temple of Mut.*

The 1850–1930s was a period of 'high imperialism' when British colonial interests in other nations was most apparent. Amelia Edwards and Margaret Benson were writing at this time and no doubt were influenced by the social and cultural aspects which permeated society. Both women however with their relatively privileged class position were able to escape the restrictions of financial and social marginalisation. Sarah Belzoni also appears to display the voice of an individual in her writing, not with independent means but with an independent mind. She began her 'account' explaining that, 'I took the opportunity while in Egypt to observe the manners of the women in that country.' In addition she always referred to her husband as 'Mr B'.

During the nineteenth century diaries, letters and journals were an ideal medium through which to express individuality. To some extent this style is reflected in the works of these three women. They were often written with humour and self-deprecation but they always had a close involvement with people and their social relationships. Possibly their opinions may have been more tentative than an imperial male voice but in this way they present an alternative view of travel and of significant archaeological discoveries.

Sarah and Maggie wrote in the first person – immediately directing the reader to their narrative and experiences. Amelia Edwards, and Margaret Benson's writings appear more dignified; they were able to afford servants and comfortable travel and the best European style hotels. Sarah's writing reflects that of many early women pioneers in the New World as opposed to the Old. Amelia Edwards writes in the third person, as 'the writer', but her style is still personal. On her discovery of Egypt she says: 'in simple truth we had drifted hither by accident, with no excuse of health or business or any serious object whatever; and had just taken refuge in Egypt … – to get out of the rain.'

In these narratives, the missing or understated comment often contributes to a fuller picture. Sarah Belzoni often experienced real physical and financial hardships, but these are stated in a matter-of-fact, down-to-earth manner. She suffered from intermittent fevers, without medicine or tea, being 'screwed up in a small boat for a month.'[18] In Cairo 'Mr B deposits her in a house, alone without an interpreter and about 20 Arab words to my mouth. Never in my life [have I] felt so isolated and miserable, in a violent fever, exposed to the burning sun, and being an object of curiosity.' She suffered from opthalmia, losing her sight for twenty days and used 'medicines provided by Christian and Mohammedan women'. This description contains realism but no self-pity.

Although Sarah Belzoni, Amelia Edwards and Margaret Benson, may at first have 'drifted' into the world of archaeology, they all, within their own parameters, had some degree of achievement. They may have been small and 'trifling', in the case of Sarah, Margaret Benson's achievements may have been short lived although she put women in the Egyptian excavational picture for the first time. Amelia Edwards, however, from an impetuous and insignificant decision to escape bad weather in Europe, by taking a boat to Alexandria, was to put the discipline of Egyptian archaeology legitimately, academically and economically on the European 'map'.

---

[18] 'Trifling Account', 416.

Bibliography

Askwith, B., *Two Victorian Families* (London, Chatto and Windus, 1971).

Baedeker, K., *Egypt and the Sudan: Handbook for Travellers* (Leipzig, 1881).

Belzoni, G., *Narrative of the Operations and Recent Discoveries within the* Pyramids, Temples, Tombs, and Excavations in Egypt and Nubia; in Search of the *Ancient Berenice and Another to the Oasis of Jupiter Ammon* (London, Murray, 1820).

Benson, M. G. K., *The Temple of Mut in Asher* (London, Murray, 1899).

Benson, M. G. K. and Gourlay, J., 'The Temple of Mut in Asher', in *KMT, Journal of Ancient Egypt* (San Francisco, 1899).

Clair, C., *Strong Man Egyptologist* (Norwich, Oldbourne, 1957).

Edwards, A., *A Thousand Miles up The Nile* (Bath, Bath Press, 1888).

Edwards, A., *Pharaohs Fellahs and Explorers* (London, Murray 1891).

Janssen, R. *The First Hundred Years: Egyptology at University College London 1892–1992.* (London, UCL Press, 1992).

Mayes, S., *The Great Belzoni* (London, Putnam, 1959).

Peck, W. H., 'Miss Benson and Mut' *KMT* 2(1) 1991: 10–19, 63–65.

Rees, J. *Amelia Edwards: Traveller, Novelist, Egyptologist* (London, Rubicon Press, 1995).

6. A Woman's Perception of Nineteenth Century Egypt: Lucie Duff Gordon

Sarah Searight

'I long to bore you with travellers' tales,' Lucie Duff Gordon wrote to her husband Alexander in 1863 in one of her memorable letters, written after her first winter in Egypt.[1] She neither bored him, however, nor did she really long to do so; Lucie's *Letters from Egypt*, first published in 1865, with three reprints the same year, were superbly crafted and intended as such, in order to pay the expenses of her sojourn in Egypt. This, it was hoped when she set off from England in 1861, would assuage the terrible effects of her tuberculosis.

There are countless books about nineteenth century Egypt – discoveries and rediscoveries, on archaeology and anthropology, the political assessment often leading to the patronisingly imperial tract. Plenty for Alexander Duff Gordon and Lucie's many other readers to choose from if they so wished. But Lucie handled her readership with an astuteness cultivated by years of literary association in England and on the continent. Her seven years in Upper Egypt were the longest any European woman had spent in that part of the world (sadly for Alexander and her children) and she put them to good use: the fresh, uniquely sympathetic but acute observations on life in her adopted country, which she made in her letters home, painted a portrait of that country dramatically different from previous accounts and from many since. The word 'dramatically' is particularly appropriate to Lucie's letters; her descriptions of her meetings with a vast range of Egyptian life often read like scenes from a play.

Lucie was born in 1821, the daughter of John and Sarah Austin, a serious-minded couple with all the right connections. John was an academic lawyer who wrote books on jurisprudence and bequeathed to Lucie that 'innate bent to

---

[1] Lucie Duff Gordon, *Letters from Egypt* (London, 1902), November 14th, 1863.

exactitude', as George Meredith put it,[2] so apparent in the letters; her mother supplemented a meagre income by translations of German literature. Their friends were radicals of the day – Bentham, John Stuart Mill, Macaulay among them – and Lucie grew up as an only and precocious child in their midst. London proving expensive the family moved to the continent, travelling in France and Germany, as a result of which she read French and German fluently; during a stay in Boulogne they were befriended by Heinrich Heine. She had a spell in a hated boarding school and at the age of eighteen met and married the handsome Scottish baronet, Alexander Duff Gordon, well connected but not so well paid as a minor Treasury employee.

They were a handsome and popular couple. Judging by her portrait by Henry Phillips, painted around 1851 (in the National Portrait Gallery) she was remarkably beautiful, Alexander her match in looks. They attracted to their Westminster house and later to Esher an intelligentsia that stood Lucie in good stead when she embarked on her literary career, initially following in her mother's footsteps as a translator. George Meredith was among their friends, much in love for a while with Lucie's elder daughter Janet and later author of a memoir of Lucie. Several other friends had travelled in the Near East – Kinglake whose *Eothen* appeared in 1834, Thackeray whose *Cornhill to Cairo* was published in 1844, Elliott Warburton whose *The Crescent and the Cross* was published in 1845. Their accounts are witty, mocking and self-deprecating, popular with the Victorian armchair traveller, still entertaining reading today and a contrast to the earnest tomes produced by such as the worthy Harriet Martineau.[3] But you would not be much the wiser about the world they travelled through; in this particular respect their approach is very different from what Lucie's was to be.

In the late 1850s Lucie developed a hacking cough, perhaps the result of nursing her dying father in a cold and damp cottage at Weybridge. One winter she nearly died of bronchitis and soon after that appeared the first signs of the dread tuberculosis. In 1860 her doctor told her she was too ill to spend the winter in England and that autumn she set sail for South Africa, leaving her family in England and writing lively letters to them about her travels. Her health was not sufficiently improved; she was warned she should on no account spend another winter in England and so the decision was taken to experiment with Egypt. The year before Janet her daughter had married Henry Ross, a middle-aged banker in Alexandria. Lucie, perhaps guided by Kinglake or Thackeray, decided she would be less cut off from family and friends if she tried wintering in Egypt.

---

[2] Meredith wrote an introduction to the 1902 edition of Lucie's *Letters*.

[3] Lucie criticised Harriet Martineau's *Eastern Life Past and Present*, published in 1843, as having excellent descriptions 'but she evidently knew and cared nothing about the people here' (February 7th, 1864).

Lucie, Lady Duff Gordon, painted by Henry Wyndham Phillips, 1851. Published courtesy of the National Portrait Gallery.

The 'unveiling' or development of modern Egypt stemmed from the French invasion in 1798 but even more from the policies of the first post-Napoleon ruler, the Viceroy (as he became) Muhammad Ali who governed the country as a semi-autonomous province of the Ottoman Empire. Muhammad Ali was a military adventurer who with European assistance remodelled the Egyptian army and administration on more European lines. This in due course brought about radical changes in the society, culture and politics of Egypt which his successors were in general unable to control. Their growing dependence on European finance replaced Ottoman rule with the far more onerous burden of British and French interference as creditors, the burden borne on the whole by the Egyptian tax payer, as Lucie frequently noted. The almost medieval city life described so vividly by Edward Lane in his *Manners and Customs of the Modern Egyptians* (published in 1836) was a far cry from the scene of rural deprivation that Lucie described.

Muhammad Ali's successors, in particular his nephew Ismail who became viceroy in 1863, just a year after Lucie's arrival, had even greater delusions of grandeur. Railways, harbours, cotton plantations, above all the Suez Canal were designed to elevate Egypt in the eyes of Europe as well as enrich the viceroy and a good many European hangers-on. Many of those who came to Egypt meant well – Lucie's son-in-law, the banker Henry Ross worked for the bank in Alexandria founded by Samuel Briggs, an entrepreneur who persuaded Muhammad Ali to introduce cotton and to improve communications between Cairo and Alexandria by excavating the Mahmudiyyah Canal (Lucie steamed along it on her initial journey to Cairo). Not all were as scrupulous as Briggs, however. On his accession to power Ismail was soon on the way to impoverishing the country irreparably. Lucie's letters are a sad commentary on this state of affairs.

She steamed across the Mediterranean in the late summer of 1861, arriving at Alexandria to find her daughter off on a hunting expedition; loathing the noise and dirt of that city Lucie soon set off for Cairo which initially she loved: 'I write to you out of the real Arabian Nights,' she wrote to her mother early in November 1861. 'Well may the Prophet (whose name be exalted) smile when he looks on Cairo. It is a golden existence – all sunshine and poetry, and I must add, kindness and civility.'[4] Sadly the city was not so kind to her health and as soon as the weather cooled she rented a Nile boat, known as a *dahabiyyah* (£25 a month, including crew) and headed upriver to Abu Simbel. It was while staying in Luxor on her voyage northwards that she first conceived the idea of living there. That summer she returned to England for a brief sickly three months; while there she was encouraged by Meredith and Alexander reluctantly to allow publication of the letters she had written from South Africa, on the grounds that it would help pay for the expenses of her Egyptian sojourn. *Letters from the Cape* was published in 1864.

Lucie's letters home thereafter, mostly from the rickety house she rented in the heart of the village that nestled in the ruins of the Great Temple of Luxor, but also from her regular visits to Cairo, are among the most acute observations of local life, and her participation in it, made by foreigners in Egypt in the nineteenth century. Her 'Theban palace' had been built into the ruins of the Temple of Luxor by that great looter of Pharaonic stones, Henry Salt, (and occupied by later generations of looters) but to Lucie 'it seems more and more beautiful,' she told her husband, 'a lovely dwelling … Some men came to mend the staircase, which had fallen in and which consists of huge solid blocks of

---

[4] November 11th, 1862.

stone.' A workman crushed a finger 'and I had to operate on it', another of Lucie's many first aid occasions.[5] Rather more of the house collapsed by the time she came to leave it.

Rare among foreigners she went to great lengths to learn Arabic. Within a few days of her arrival in Cairo she had mastered a few words of colloquial Arabic, then in Luxor she acquired a teacher for the classical language. 'Oh dear what must poor Arab children suffer in learning A B C,' she wrote later,[6] complaining of the difficulty of writing backwards. But speaking Arabic obviously made all the difference to her relations with all those around her: she tended the sick, dined with the local great and good, listened to complaints, and at times of famine and cattle disease (both frequent misfortunes) fed all and sundry. Knowing the language was crucial to her understanding of the problems around her. 'One must come to the East to understand absolute equality,' she wrote with upper-class confidence; 'money and rank are looked on as mere accidents, and my *savoir vivre* was highly thought of because I sat down with Fellaheen and treated everyone as they treat each other.'[7] John Stuart Mill would surely have approved.

She was attended throughout by a faithful servant, Omar. In April 1864, the hottest time of year, she sailed upriver to Philae, which she like most European visitors adored. Omar tended her against heat exhaustion and sang sad Turkish songs, but '"Do not rub my feet, oh Brother, that is not fit for thee,"' she told him to which he responded, '"The slave of the Turk may be set free by money but how shall one be ransomed who has been paid for by kind actions and sweet words".' And she even forgave Omar when her almost as faithful maid Sally gave birth to Omar's child. The maid was dismissed; Omar stayed.

One relishes too the descriptions of her shaikhly visitors, one of whom was her teacher Shaikh Yusuf, 'a graceful, sweet-looking young man, with a dark brown face and such fine manners', 'a perfect darling'. Interest in the language of Islam encouraged an interest in the faith itself: visits to mosques, to saints' shrines, attending feasting at the end of Ramadhan. She attends the departure of the *mahmal*, the covering for the Kaabah in Mecca, and the *hajj* or pilgrimage heading from Cairo also to Mecca – 'all those men prepared to endure such hardship.'[8] Her role treating the sick was particularly important: 'Yesterday was Bairam [the feast at the end of the Muslim month of fasting] – she writes – I rejoice to say and I have lots of physic to make up, for all the stomachs damaged by Ramadan.'[9] On one occasion she runs out of medicines, including Epsom

---

[5] January 13th, 1864.
[6] November 21st, 1866.
[7] May 12th, 1863.
[8] April 13th, 1863.
[9] April 1865.

salts. She writes of her tolerance of the petitions for help, her readiness to respond to the petitions, of the tolerance of her Muslim friends towards a Christian, though found the Copts less sympathetic. She attends harvest festival, a great celebration when the harvest is good as it was that year.

She also tells tourists not to shoot pigeons which are private property (housed of course in those splendid pigeon houses which are such a feature of the Egyptian landscape); in 1906 such shooting at Dinshawai in the Delta would develop into a major political incident. Tourists are generally less welcome, especially after the publication of the first batch of Egypt letters in 1865 turned her into a celebrity; the women always want to borrow Lucie's side saddle rather than make do with the local saddle: 'last year five women on one steamer all sent for my saddle, besides other things – campstools, umbrellas, beer etc. etc.'[10] Particularly important is the fact that as a woman she could make friends, and did, among the local women; medicines, her Arabic and her sex were an invaluable combination.

She did like certain visitors: Edward Lear was 'a pleasant man and I was glad to see him',[11] the artist Marianne Moore and her father, the Prince and Princess of Wales whom she liked, especially the princess – 'the most perfectly simple-mannered girl I ever saw', the prince too, 'quite respectful in his manner', as well he might be, given Lucie's reputation (but also extreme fragility) at the time of their visit in 1869.[12] Above all her ne'er-do-well son Maurice whose manners are so much improved by consorting with the locals. There's a poignant moment as she says goodbye to Maurice just a month before her death, for he mustn't think of coming out again, 'he must begin work now or he will never be good for anything.' Right to the end Lucie remained a most artful letter writer.

She was unique in another significant respect, the one European to note the effect of the Khedive Ismail's commitment to the construction of the Suez Canal on the rural population of Egypt. This major construction project demanded not only a huge increase in taxation but also a vast workforce, extracted from the countryside by a forced levy known as the *corvée*. 'Everyone is cursing the French here,' she wrote on February 11th 1863. 'Forty thousand men always at work on the Suez Canal at starvation point does not endear them to the project.'[13] Ismail was forced to abolish the system before the completion of the canal but not before Lucie had reported the appalling impact on the countryside. The radicalism of her childhood comes to mind: 'I should like to see person and property safe which no one's here is (Europeans of course excepted),' she wrote to her mother. 'Food … gets dearer and the forced labour

---

[10] January 22nd, 1867.
[11] *Ibid.*
[12] February 11th, 1869.
[13] January 9th, 1864.

inflicts more suffering.' She goes on: 'What chokes me is to hear English people talk of the stick being "the only way to manage the Arabs", as if any one could doubt that it is the *easiest* way to manage any people where it can be used with impunity.'[14] In 1867 she wrote to Alexander (February 5th), 'I cannot describe to you the misery here now, indeed it is wearisome to think of: every day some new tax', and later the same year she compared an earlier view from her window (of 'the lovely smiling landscape') with the 'dreary waste now' before her.

Lucie's story, like that of so many consumptives in the nineteenth century, is as poignant to us today as it was to her contemporaries – far from family, far from a husband who showed no great anguish for her plight, surrounded by local people who adored her. Lucie's penultimate letter to her husband easily reddens eyes, written from Boulak on the Nile outside Cairo on June 15th, 1869, a month before her death:

> Dearest Alick,
> Do not think of coming here. Indeed it would be almost too painful to me to part from you again; and as it is, I can patiently wait for the end among people who are kind and loving enough to be comfortable, without too much feeling of the pain of parting…

And on July 9th, just four days before dying:

> I wish I had seen your dear face once more – but not now, I would not have you here now on any account…

Such a farewell casts quite a spell and was intended to do so; it does Lucie no harm to suggest that was indeed her intention. It is a spell that has lasted a hundred and fifty years, since the first edition of letters, those of 1863–65, edited by Alexander and Lucie's mother, Sarah Austin, was published in 1865 and reprinted three times that year. A revised and enlarged edition, with a memoir by Lucie's daughter Janet and a new introduction by George Meredith, was published in 1902. A third edition edited by Gordon Waterfield (a long-time English resident in Egypt) was published in 1969; I edited a fourth edition for Virago in 1983 and a fifth was edited by Lucie's superb biographer, Katherine Frank, in 1994. As Ms Frank acknowledges in her biography, the *Letters* are sold 'in almost every bookshop up and down the Nile … so that Lucie Duff Gordon is almost as much of a name to reckon with in contemporary Egypt as she was when besieged by officious tourists' in Luxor. Together with Edward Lane's *Manners and Customs of the Modern Egyptians*, the *Letters from Egypt* of Lucie Duff Gordon are essential reading for anyone taking up residence in, or travelling amongst, Egyptian society today. Of the women in this volume, how many of them have survived so well in their writings? Possibly only that other inveterate letter writer, Lady Mary Wortley Montagu.

---

[14] January 5th, 1864.

On the face of it Lucie does not seem to have a hand in the editing of the *Letters*; initially this seems to have been done by her husband and mother in London, subsequently by her daughter Janet Ross. It would therefore have been her family who selected the passages most suitable for publication and on the whole one respects their choice, even their emphasis on Lucie's ill health. This intrudes at regular intervals, enhancing the pathos of the story. Without wishing to down-play the tuberculosis, it is all part of the essential crafting behind the publication and accounts at least partly for its lasting success.

There are advantages to being a woman such as Lucie in a world where men and women were, and largely still are, content to lead separate lives, into both of which she could enter. I have often been asked: 'What is it like, travelling, working in the Muslim world?', to which I can only say that as a woman I am treated with great politeness and respect by the men of that world as well as being warmly welcomed by the women. Lucie's letters are a constant reminder of the same, of how successfully she entered into both worlds, speaking the language, offering consolation and first aid. And she was particularly intrigued by 'an eccentric Bedawee lady' whom she met in 1864, dressed like a young man; 'her manner was excellent, not the least impudent or swaggering … She is … fond of travelling and of men's society, being very clever, so she has her dromedary and goes about quite alone.'[15] Not so very different from Lucie herself.

Travel literature is much in vogue today, covering table after table in the bookshops. Lucie herself made an interesting comment on travel literature, writing on February 7th 1864 to her mother 'that all the old books of travel that I have read mention the natives of strange countries in a far more natural tone, and with far more attempt to discriminate character, than modern ones.' She goes on: 'Modern travellers show strange ignorance in talking of foreign natives *in the* lump.' That certainly doesn't apply to Lucie herself. Through her letters – so fresh today – we get to know so many of her characters – her teacher Shaikh Yusuf, her devoted servant Omar, Mustafa Agha the rich Luxor merchant and consular agent, the Ababdah shaikhs, and a whole host of lesser mortals. She was as much at home with the men as with the women but took a special pleasure in her familiarity with *harim* life. European women visitors to the Muslim world took it for granted that they should take an interest in the women's world of the *harim* but Lucie's Arabic placed her on a unique footing with the women of the household. Our pleasure in reading her letters is the result of her craft and perhaps too that of her editors. On the whole, however, I would give her the benefit of the doubt and assume it was she whose crafting was so meticulous, even on her death bed. Lucie's upbringing and social circle ensured that she was more than just well read; through her work as translator she could

---

[15] February 11th, 1863.

handle the subtleties and nuances of description, particularly of the people by whom she was surrounded in Luxor. She has the almost hypnotising perception of Elizabeth Gaskell or Jane Austen. Clearly she was more interested in people than in the Pharaonic ruins with which she was surrounded, descriptions of which cover so many less enduring pages on overladen library shelves; we benefit as a result. She was bewitched, as we all are, by the 'sacred Nile' beside which she was privileged to live, and by 'the perfect freshness of the gigantic buildings, the beauty of the sculptures,' amongst which she lived, above all by 'the charm of the people'.

Taking 'travel literature' in general, such a popular genre today, I would suggest that too large a part of it is subjective, telling the reader more about the author, the traveller, than about the people and places travelled amongst. Conversations in the first person are a poor substitute for in-depth description; this criticism can also be applied to the television travelogue where the presenter has a far higher profile than those he presents. The popularity of the genre is directly the result of the fact that, contrary to their image of themselves, the British are not great travellers; in exotic arenas they are always outnumbered by other nationalities. They prefer their British armchairs; thank goodness Lucie was happiest in her ramshackle house in the Luxor temple, a traveller who could truly relate to her adopted home.

Bibliography

Duff Gordon, Lucie, *Letters from Egypt 1863–65* ed. Sarah Austin, her mother (London, Macmillan, 1865).

Frank, Kathleen, *Lucie Duff Gordon: A Passage to Egypt* (London, Hamish Hamilton, 1994).

Letters from Egypt, revised by and with memoir by her daughter Janet Ross and New introduction by George Meredith (London, 1902).

Letters from Egypt ed. Gordon Waterfield (London, Routledge & Kegan Paul, 1969).

Letters from Egypt ed. Sarah Searight (London, Virago, 1983).

Letters from Egypt ed. Kathleen Frank (London, Virago, 1997).

7. Governess to the Grand Pasha of Egypt: Emmeline Lott

Alix Wilkinson

Governesses were always in a difficult social position, being lone women, dependent on the households in which they worked. Emmeline Lott was one such woman, who became governess to the children of foreign royalty and nobility. She went to Egypt in 1863 to look after the five-year old son, Ibrahim, of Ismail Pasha (viceroy of Egypt from 1863 to 1879), and recorded her experiences in three books. One is an account of life in Ismail's *harim*.[1] The second is a two-volume description of a voyage on the Nile, in his yacht, visiting dignitaries and antiquities along the way.[2] And the third is a novel about life in the *harim* and stories told by the characters in the novel.[3]

Her reason for going to Egypt is not evident from her writings, although she presumably needed to earn some money. The 1860s was a time when women were in surplus, and for whom the Female Middle Class Emigration Society was founded in 1862 to provide loans to women who wished to emigrate to the colonies.[4] But she had been married, as her contract with her publisher shows,[5] so she may have been widowed. Agents for the Viceroy in London arranged for her employment. She discussed her contract again in Cairo, when she stipulated that it was to be for two years only, with an escape clause if she fell ill.

---

[1] Emmeline Lott, *The English Governess in Egypt. Harem Life in Egypt and Constantinople* (London, 1866).

[2] Emmeline Lott, *The Grand Pacha's Cruise on the Nile in the Viceroy of Egypt's Yacht* (London, T. Cautley Newby, 1869).

[3] Emmeline Lott, *The Mohaddetyn in the Palace of Gezira. Nights in the Harem* (London, Chapman and Hall, 1867).

[4] Patricia Clarke, *Letters from the Colonies. The Governess 1842–1882* (London, Hutchinson, 1985).

[5] British Library, Add. 46618.f.80 Bentley Papers.

She may already have had experience of living in the East, since she refers to beating the tattoo in India, sepoys drinking 'bang', and the prawns in the Ganges which fed on human corpses. She also described a banking game which the child Ibrahim played, in which he was a 'dealer in rupees', the Indian currency. A childhood home seems to have been Windsor, where she played in the private royal grounds, and encountered Queen Victoria and Prince Albert. She mentions Wales in a reference to the state of the road between Haverford West and St. David's.

She says her purpose in writing about her *harim* experiences was to correct the misapprehensions about them current in England. She compares her intimate and daily experience of the *harim*, with the writings of Lady Mary Wortley Montagu, who had 'not the slightest opportunity to study the daily life of the Odalisques, for she never penetrated beyond reception halls, swept garnished for her reception.' Nor did Lucie Duff Gordon, who contrasts her own visit to a *harim*, which was 'not a bit like the description in Mrs Lott's most extraordinary book.'[6] But Emmeline may have started out with romantic ideas based on Tom Moore's *Lalla Rookh*, which she quotes in her first book. This narration and poem, published in 1817, is a highly idealised description of the charms of *harim* ladies. It ran to many printed editions, with a variety of illustrations, such as that by the Corbaux sisters in 1837, who wished to render 'those bright creations of the poet's fancy as familiar to the eye, as they are already to the mind and to the heart.'[7] Opinions about *harim* life in Egypt ranged from those who believed the women lived a life of unimaginable luxury and ease, to those who thought it was a vicious form of slavery. Jean-Jacques Ampère (son of the famous physicist whose own *Voyage en Égypte et en Nubie* was published in 1867) opted for a middle way: 'the women are not recluses but separate from men.'[8]

Emmeline arrived in Alexandria in 1863, when Ismail had just become ruler. In the first-class carriage on the train to Cairo from Alexandria, she was intrigued by a train-load of young women, described as His Highness' private dispatches by the railway authorities. She fell into conversation with a Greek merchant and a German Jew. Her travelling companions were very worried that, 'any English lady should have accepted the appointment you have,' and the Greek said: 'I urge you to abandon the idea of entering His Highness's service.' One reason was they felt she would not understand the system of *bakshish*. She had read about 'Prince Baksheesh, without whose aid very little can be done', in a magazine called *Once a Week*.[9] Had she heeded this warning, and the article in

---

[6] Lucie Duff Gordon, *Letters from Egypt 1862–1869 by Lady Duff Gordon,* ed. Gordon Waterfield (London, Routledge and Kegan Paul, 1969).

[7] Drawings to accompany *Pearls of the East or beauties from Lalla Roukh,* designed by Fanny Corbaux (London, Charles Tilt, 1837).

[8] J. J. Ampère, *Voyage en Égypte et en Nubie* (Paris, Michel Lévy, 1868), 185–6.

[9] *Once a Week* (September 1, 1860), 267–72.

the same magazine by Harriet Martineau on the subject of governesses, she might have saved herself much distress. But even worse was the peculiar diet of the 'Caged Birds of the Abode of Bliss', which would be 'unpalatable and injurious to your health'. The women 'drink acqua vita and the air is polluted with tobacco.'

The people in Cairo responsible for her employment were Mr. B., who may have been Bravay, an 'ingratiating charlatan', representative of Rothschilds.[10] The other was a Prussian, Mr. C. of H., whom she describes as a 'Crimean suttler'. She also mentions Oppenheim's Bank. Henry Oppenheim provisioned the British army in the Crimean War. Oppenheims then became bankers to Ismail Pasha and loaned him large sums of money.[11] Oppenheim had a sumptuous villa on the Shubra road, constructed in part by Carl von Diebitsch, who provided the ironwork for Ismail's Gezira palace.[12] She refers to her employers as the 'Frankfort clique', and to Messrs. H. as the 'genii of the Abodes of Bliss'. She makes much play with these colourful names for the *harim* and its inhabitants.

The *harim* occupied the site of the two Baehler mansions on the north side of the present day July 26 Street in Zamalek.[13] When she arrived she was received by the Chief Eunuch, a very tall man, who passed her on to the 'Lady Superintendent', who took her to the child's mother, in a room overlooking the Nile. This 'wee dwarf of a handsome blonde' with plaited hair was a Circassian, called Djananiar, and Ismail Pasha's second wife. She had charge of Ibrahim's upbringing, and issued erratic orders about when the child should go for walks. Early on she suggested to Emmeline that she should discipline the boy by sticking him with a hair pin, advice she wisely ignored, although she found she could threaten him with them. His Highness the Grand Pasha Ibrahim, Ismail's fourth son, was a heavy-looking, violent, greedy little boy, given to un-controllable, and uncontrolled, outbursts of rage. On one occasion he threw a shovel full of hot coals at a slave who disturbed him by chattering. On another, he ordered the gardeners who had spent too long gathering some flowers for him, to be flogged in his presence. He attacked his playmates, and tore the flesh off the inside cheeks of a child who had displeased him, 'until the blood streamed down her chin like water.'

---

[10] David S. Landes, *Bankers and Pashas. International finance and economic imperialism in Egypt* (London, Heinemann, 1958).

[11] Richard Annesley, *The Rise of Modern Egypt* (Edinburgh, Pentland Press, 1994), 161.

[12] Elke Pflugradt-Abdel Aziz, *A Prussian Palace in Egypt. Exhibition Catalogue, Museum of Egyptian Modern Arts. October 16 – November 13* (Cairo, Museum of Egyptian Modern Arts, 1993), 15.

[13] Samir Raafat, *Cairo Times* October 14th, 1999 and December 15th, 2000.

Emmeline Lott wearing formal Turkish outdoor dress. Portrait in her first book, 'The English Governess in Egypt. Harem Life in Egypt and Constantinople' (London 1866). Reproduced by kind permission of The British Library.

Emmeline first encountered Ismail Pasha in his dressing gown and slippers and mistook him for the barber. He was always cordial in his dealings with her. And, as she learnt too late, he had ordered that her quarters and meals should be greatly improved. He was certainly not lewd with her, as has been suggested.[14]

---

[14] Patricia D. Netzley, *The Encyclopedia of Women's Travel and Exploration* (Westport, CT, Oryx, 2001).

The First Wife directed the household, which functioned through a hierarchy of slaves, under the control of the Grand Eunuch. Slavery was supposed to have been abolished by this time, but as Ismail informed Sir Bartle Frere (later to be involved in the suppression of the East African slave trade) in 1872, domestic slavery was 'impossible to stop', although Ismail had backed British attempts to end slavery in East Africa, as part of his plan to annex the Sudan.[15] The household consisted of the Pasha's three wives, the favourites, *ikbals*, and their children, served by a staff of slaves. There were about one hundred and fifty to two hundred people in the *harim*. The women spent their days dressed in filthy, crumpled muslin dresses, 'like slatterns of St. Giles, smoking, and drinking coffee'. They consumed opium, hemp (cannabis), and *kef*, which was distilled hemp, 'haschachir'[sic], which produced delusions, and, to Emmeline's surprise, wine. Although they washed from a bowl every day, they accumulated fleas and other creatures, which they combed out of their hair once a week. One royal child had lost all its hair to infestations and had to wear a tarboosh. Only when a visit by the Pasha was announced did the women put on the elegant clothes and splendid jewellery which he had given them. But there were at least two bathrooms, one for Ismail and one for Ibrahim's mother, which was only used 'after visits to the viceroy'. The woman chosen by the Pasha as that night's companion, was washed, perfumed and arrayed in finery, before being sent over to his elegant kiosk in the grounds, accompanied by musicians. She walked with a shuffling gait, common to most of the women in the *harim*. This could have been due to their footwear, or to their having been circumcised, rather than sitting cross-legged.[16] The *harim* was a hotbed of intrigue and jealousy. The Pasha feared that his son would be poisoned, and the boy's nurse did indeed try to poison Emmeline.

The appearance and habits of the African slaves shocked Emmeline. She refers to the eunuchs as 'spectres'. The noise of chatter in many languages, none of which she could at first understand, irritated her. But she says she 'picked up' both Arabic and Turkish in a very short space of time and could evidently hold a polite conversation with the royal ladies.

A dinner party could be a splendid affair, but the system of feeding the household was a free for all. The food for the royalty was brought from the kitchens outside the *harim*, and left in the stone hall on the ground floor. As soon as it was put down, and before being collected by the appropriate servants, the slaves descended on it, and grabbed what they could, before it was taken to its intended destination. The royal children's nurses stole the food from their charges during breakfast. Emmeline hated the food provided in the *harims*. In

---

[15] Reda Mowafi, *Slavery, slave trade and abolition attempts in Egypt and the Sudan, 1820–1882* (Lund Studies, Lund, 1981), 69.

[16] James Clough, *Oriental Orgies* (London, Anthony Blond, 1968), 79.

Cairo it was kebabs, burnt to a cinder, dry Arab bread and coffee. In Constantinople, where the family went on holiday, she lived on bread, fruit and pigeon, 'being the only eatables that approached to anything like a European diet'.

Her room in Cairo, twelve feet square, was off the child's bedroom. A redeeming feature was that it overlooked the garden, and the kiosk in its centre, but it lacked most furniture, even a 'vase', or chamber-pot, and she had to 'do battle' in Cairo and in Constantinople for furniture and other necessities. Her main duty was to be with Ibrahim all the time, and never to leave him alone. Emmeline thought at first that she was to undertake his general instruction. Later, the Pasha told her that she should teach him English, but without using books or toys. Then both he and his wives told her, 'not to care about his instruction'. At this she began to worry that the real purpose of her being there was that she should become a 'Favourite'. She was indeed so accused by the *harim* ladies. Only the honesty of her little charge, which they all respected, on the subject of a visit to the Pasha in his bedroom, made them realise that she was not the new *ikbal* and she was saved from being murdered. For her part, she says she had 'no idea of passing the best years of my existence within a "gilded cage"'. Emmeline was fortunate in being able to leave the *harim* and take her charge to visit other members of the royal family, such as the widow of Ismail's uncle and previous Viceroy Muhammad Said Pasha at Shubra, and the Grand Princess and the Petite Princess, wives of Hamil Pasha, another of Ismail's uncles. Madame de Gasparin had also visited the household in 1847–8, before Muhammed Ali died.[17]

Emmeline became ill in Constantinople and wanted a break from her duties, but was forced by the palace officials to resign, although she was eager to continue. Dr. Ogilvie, doctor to the British consul, Mr. Colquhoun,[18] recommended rest and treatment, but 'Mr. H. [the banker] refused to let me leave the palace unless I resigned my post.'

It is not clear why she wanted to stay, since she was ill and complained about her 'unprofitable, irksome and thankless task' as governess. It is doubtful if she was paid, since she says, 'I have asked for my just rights since my return to Europe, but they have not been accorded to me.' She never managed to make anything out of the *bakshish* system which perhaps was intended as her pay. She was ill for much of her time in Cairo, and even contracted cholera. She disliked the food, and ate only bread, broth and sweetmeats all during her stay. She was

---

[17] Mme. de Gasparin, *Journal d'un voyage au Levant* (Paris, Marc Duclous, 1848), 460.

[18] Sir Robert Gilmour Colquhoun, 1804–1870, was appointed Consul-General in Egypt in December 1858 and resigned in 1865. Warren R. Dawson, Eric P. Uphill, *Who was Who in Egyptology,* 3rd. ed by Morris Bierbrier (London, Egypt Exploration Society, 1995).

plagued by fleas, cockroaches and mosquitoes. The *harims* were filthy. Her quarters were cramped and mean. The 'conversation of the Odalisques was most indelicate', their topics 'criminal, indecent, filthy and disgusting'. Those in charge of the household neglected her needs and took no care of her when she was seriously ill. She does not seem to have made any friends in the *harim*. She felt herself superior to the other employees, especially the German laundry-maid, who ate with her at the beginning of her stay. Ibrahim's nurse, Shaytan, an African, was jealous of her and hostile to the point of attempting her murder. Fortunately the boy's mother 'always treated me like a sister.' Ibrahim, when questioned, told Said Pasha's widow that he liked her. And she maintained that she had 'gained the confidence and respect of all, through being an adviser on all subjects to the inmates.'

Because she lived in the *harim*, she had no contacts with any British or other Europeans in Cairo, although she implies that she attended Divine Service. Ironically, her persecutor, Oppenheim, had converted to Anglicanism.[19] The only foreigners she mentions are the bankers and her predecessor, Miss T., who had been dismissed for visiting the *harim* of Muhammad Said Pasha and accused of peeping and prying into other *harims*. So she was deprived of information which could have been useful to her, and of the companionship which other foreigners in Cairo in the 1860s enjoyed. Her most enthusiastic descriptions are of the splendour and luxury of Ismail's residences. She gives detailed accounts of the palaces of Gezira: the kiosk in the garden, where the Anglican Cathedral now stands,[20] and the main building by the Nile which has been incorporated into the Marriott Hotel. She enjoyed walking in the garden at Gezira when it was not too hot. The trips on the Nile were a particular pleasure. She was excited by the sights and sounds of Cairo when she went out on rare visits to other family members, such as Ismail's mother, who lived in the Citadel. At the palace at Ras al-Tin in Alexandria she enjoyed the sea breezes but was uncomfortable in every other way, and the palaces in Constantinople were frightening. Constantinople thrilled her and she spent many hours in the grounds of the palace there with Ibrahim, tasting the fruit from the trees, admiring the views and going for boat trips on the Bosphorus.

Emmeline arrived at a bad time in Egypt's fortunes: a mysterious disease had killed most of the cattle; then there was a great flood. In 1863 food prices rose sharply and in 1864, with the end of the Civil War in the United States, cotton prices fell so disastrously that Ismail refused to sell his crop, thereby denying himself much needed income.

In due course she returned to England, and lived in Brighton writing her first book, which was republished three years running, in spite of getting hostile

---

[19] Elke Pflugradt-Abdel Aziz, *op. cit.*, 15.
[20] Samir Raafat, *Cairo Times,* December 15th, 2000.

The Guard of the Seraglio' by Jean Lecomte du Noüy, said to have been based on Emmeline Lott's description of the harim at Gezira. Courtesy Collection Yves Saint Laurent-Pierre Bergé.

reviews in American papers.[21] She may have taken up employment with the Duke of Rutland, since *The Grand Pacha's Cruise on the Nile* is dedicated to His Grace, Charles Cecil Manners, 6th Duke of Rutland, 'for kindness received at your hands', but she is not recorded among the residents at Belvoir Castle in the census for 1871. Nor was she at her former address in Brighton, 16 Upper Rock Gardens, where in the 1861 Census, two former governesses are recorded as visitors.

The messages of her book are aimed at two different audiences. One is the European and British reader who had a fanciful view of oriental *harims*. And the other is Ismail himself, whom she wishes to warn of the 'baleful influence of *harims* on children'. She suggests that they should, be removed from the *harim* and placed with their nurse under the care of a European, with European staff, and have an establishment suitable to their rank. Another message was that foreign staff should not be housed in the *harim*. Ismail apparently heeded this

---

[21] Michael Wojcik, 'Emmeline Lott', in *Dictionary of Literary Biography* Vol. 166. *British Travel Writers 1837–1875,* edited by Barbara Brothers and Julia Gergits (Detroit, 1996).

suggestion for when Ellen Chennells, the governess for his daughter, Zeynab, arrived in 1871 she lived with the family of the newly arrived tutor, Mr. Freeland, and another teacher, Mr. Michell. They all had their own suites, but shared meals and servants. Ibrahim, his sister, and their companions, had their lessons at the tutors' house in Shubra everyday, which was 'spacious and handsome'.[22]

Emmeline Lott's account of life in a *harim* is one of a very few published by an inmate, and contrasts with those written by the women born to such a life.[23] These women also give detailed descriptions of the furnishings, dress and social customs, and provide a background against which to read European comments. European women visited *harims* for a few hours and saw inside the houses and met some of the residents. But most did not speak the languages or experience the details of life, although they imagined much. Emmeline Lott's account is valuable not only for its picture of *harim* life, but also for the insights it provides into Ismail's personality and lifestyle, and some of the political restraints under which he was operating.

---

[22] Ellen Chennells, *Recollections of an Egyptian Princess by her English governess* (London, Blackwood, 1893).

[23] Hanum Djaridan, *Harim Life* (London, Noel Douglas, 1931); Leyla Saz, *The Imperial harim of the Sultans. Memoirs of Layla Saz. Daily Life At the Ciragan Palace during the Nineteenth Century* (Istanbul, Pera, 1994).

8. The Unknown Pilgrimage to Sinai: Isabella Bird

Deborah Manley

Isabella Bird is perhaps the archetype of intrepid lady travellers. Pat Barr's biography – *A Curious Life for a Lady: The Story of Isabella Bird, Traveller Extraordinary*, published in 1970 but re-issued in 1984, and the Virago Press re-issue of Isabella's books in 1980 – brought Miss Bird to the attention of a new generation. Her *A Lady's Life in the Rocky Mountains* is usually in print somewhere nowadays and she wrote many more accounts of her travels – all still readily available to modern readers.[1] Yet the journey I introduce here is almost unknown. It was an eighteen-day pilgrimage from Cairo to St Catherine's Convent at Mount Sinai. Her biographer Pat Barr dismissed it in four lines:

> On her way home from the Golden Chersonese (the Malay Peninsula) Isabella stopped at Cairo where she contracted a fever; while still weak, she went off to camp on the slopes of Mount Sinai for four nights alone; she developed pleurodynia [rheumatism of the chest muscles].[2]

No more.

Her earlier biographer and acquaintance, Anna Stoddart, recorded very little more.[3] In Cairo, Isabella had been…

> … attacked by typhoid fever, not fully developed until she was in the desert where she had to suffer the agonies of thirst and excesses of fever-heat and shivering untended. But she made good use of its intervals and carried out a long-cherished plan of encamping on the solemn slope of Mount Sinai, spending four days in its solitude, amongst its awe-inspiring associations.

---

[1] For Isabella Bird's works see Bibliography.
[2] Barr, *A Curious Life for a Lady* (London, 1970), 182.
[3] Stoddart, *The Life of Isabella Bird* (1906), 108.

Anna Stoddart's paragraph is a brilliant précis of Isabella's journey, but why her main biographers otherwise ignored this journey I do not know.

How did I come across the pilgrimage? Prince Ibrahim Hilmy, a descendant of the great Pasha of Egypt, Muhammad Ali, spent years in exile in Britain compiling a massive bibliography of writings about *Egypt from ancient times to 1885*; included is an entry in the supplement: Bishop, Isabella, A Pilgrimage to Sinai, *The Leisure Hour*, February 1886. I knew that Isabella Bird became Mrs Bishop so I went to the Bodleian and called up the large 1886 volume of that popular journal. There was Miss Bird's account, day by day and often hour by hour, in four parts, from February 1886.[4] The account was illustrated – partly by the Anglican minister, editor and travel writer and topographical illustrator, the Reverend Samuel Manning, whose work illustrated his own and other Eastern travel accounts and other *Leisure Hour* articles.[5]

Her journey to Sinai at Eastertide 1879 was not a casual adventure. It was a true pilgrimage to the sites of the Old Testament that she knew so well from her Bible reading throughout her life. Unlike many male scholar-travellers of the period,[6] Isabella claimed 'no special interest in the actual localities occupied by the Israelites', although, as she trailed across the desert landscape and climbed to the mountain peaks, she could not help but link what she saw to the Bible, and she read large sections of the Old Testament as she rode along on her camel. She knew on her first night that 'Moses had looked up at just such moonlight as this on the night of the heaping of the waters.'

This detailed knowledge of the Bible – which Victorians assumed in their readers – gave their travel in the Holy Land a dimension that most of us can no longer share. I am sure that few of the crowding travellers we see today when we visit St Catherine's Monastery in Sinai have any real idea of why they are there. (I was lucky: a pilgrimage party from Nigeria was there with us and I talked with them briefly. They could have given me many Biblical references and certainly they had a sense of awe and history not shared by the back-packers.)

Isabella was not well when she set out from Cairo. She was still suffering from shivering and 'nausea and curious pains'. Enough to keep most of us nowadays close to base. The first miles of her journey to Suez would have been by train – though she does not mention this mundane fact; Harriet Martineau's party travelling by camel in 1847 had to add four days to the journey from Cairo

---

[4] *The Leisure Hour,* February – May, 1886.

[5] Samuel Manning, *Land of the Pharaohs, Egypt and Sinai* (London, 1875).

[6] The Biblical scholar-travellers of this period included many clergymen: the American, the Reverend Edward Robinson, Dean Stanley, W. M. Thomson D. D. author of *The Land and the Book* (London, 1887) (which does not cover Sinai), Samuel Birch, Keeper of Oriental Antiquities at the British Museum 1865–85.

to Suez.[7] The opening words of Isabella's first article give a great sense of her relief at escaping from Cairo. 'It was a striking change from the jabber and clatter of the Cairene streets to the silence and decay of Suez, and from the green fields and crops of the Nile valley to the yellow sands of the desert, and of the intensely blue waters of the sea misnamed red.' Isabella had followed her Murray's *Handbook*'s advice and set up arrangements for camels and provisions at Suez on her way through the Red Sea to Cairo a few weeks before. She briefly acknowledged three gentlemen (staff of the Peninsula and Oriental Shipping Company) who accompanied her first days, but her account really begins when she set off with a local shaikh as guide, four camels, four beduin and an Arab servant, from the Well of Moses (Ain Musa, east of the Red Sea), having been assured that the journey might be undertaken alone by 'a lady without any real risk'.

As her luxury she had packed a folding chair. Her books were the Bible, Murray's *Handbook* and *The Imitation of Christ*. Her contract with the shaikh was for eighteen days' travel – a far more serious venture than Pat Barr's 'four days camping on the slopes of Mount Sinai'. She carried a white umbrella to shelter her from the sun.

Had she read Harriet Martineau's *Eastern Life Present and Past* on crossing Sinai in 1847, beyond the points reproduced in Murray, she might have been more fearful. 'I would never say a word,' Harriet warned, 'to encourage a woman to travel in the Desert, if she must do it on the back of a camel. If she can walk, as I do, all well and good.'[8]

Disregarding Murray's advice, Isabella took, as provisions, only two tins of condensed milk, two of cocoa-and-milk, some raisins, some flour, a pot of raspberry jam, some rice and Leibig's meat extract, which had recently been developed as a food supplement. This diet she had found 'amply sufficient for the support of strength while leading an open-air life.' She supplemented it with grapes. A goat-skin filled with Nile water and the desert springs would slake her thirst. And, in case of need, she took some brandy and a few simple medicines. In this she had taken the *Handbook's* advice, provided by Captain H. S. Palmer, a member of the 1868–9 survey of the Sinai Peninsula. 'Such a goat-skin or girbeh looks,' he said, 'like a small black pig which has met a watery grave.' The water from it was noted for its 'villainous taste' and 'strong purgative properties.' 'Water,' the *Handbook* advised, 'should never be drunk alone, but always mixed with a little brandy.'[9]

On her second day Isabella met six American clergymen coming the other way with eleven baggage camels. One camel was carrying the remains of their

---

[7] Martineau, *Eastern Life Past and Present* (Philadelphia, 1908), 292.
[8] Martineau, *ibid.,* 298.
[9] Murray, *Handbook to Egypt* (London, Murray, 1873), 271.

provisions: claret, a coop of hens and a sheep. This American expedition sounds rather more like Harriet Martineau's journey, on which their cook provided three cooked meals a day, starting at five in the morning with a breakfast of hashed mutton, eggs and toast, all cooked on a trivet set in the ground. At dinner there was 'always some nice pudding or fruit pie, excellent cheese, and a dessert of oranges or capital figs.'[10]

On April 7th, 1879, near Ain Musa (the Well of Moses) two miles from her landing place on the Red Sea, and some believe the place where the Israelites landed, Isabella took almost childish pleasure in seeing her long shadow lie in purple on the crimsoning sands of the evening, though she was slightly discomforted by a nearby caravan of armed beduin.

The hardships of the journey increased as the days went by. Her seventh day from Cairo was bad. It was 105° and more – unusually hot for April. The symptoms of the illness with which she had set out had increased to include a rash which developed into blisters, a headache and bad eyes. She found sleep impossible. The hardships of the journey became 'only just endurable'. Yet to turn back was worse than to go on – and 'the glorious desert – the new rich experience and the prospect of Sinai made it all seem worthwhile.'

When one reads such words, one must wonder who was this indomitable Victorian lady traveller who set out effectively on her own with such assurance? She was born in Yorkshire in 1831 and was brought up in English villages. But after the death of her father she lived in Edinburgh and on the west coast island of Mull most of the rest of her life. She was, in 1879, forty-eight years old and a spinster (though soon to marry a Scottish doctor and become Mrs John Bishop). She had travelled in America and Canada by road and rail in her early twenties – and written a very funny book about her experiences;[11] she had travelled in the Pacific, and up and down the Rocky Mountains on horseback. She had been in Japan and China and was returning now from five weeks in the Malay peninsula.

Most of her life she had had a serious back problem and often suffered from what one biographer described as 'spinal prostration'. Anna Stoddart, who first met her in her thirties, described her as 'a small woman, with great, observant eyes, flashing and smiling, but melancholy when she was silent... Her voice was soft and perfectly modulated ... but so magnetic that all in the room were absorbed in listening to her.' Another acquaintance commented that 'she had a refined humour, intellectual power,... and a dignity that forebade the slightest approach to familiarity.'[12]

[10] Martineau, *op. cit.*, 296.
[11] *An Englishwoman in America*, 1856.
[12] Stoddart, *op. cit.*, 49.

Isabella was, obviously, a very tough lady. But even for her Good Friday in the desert was terrible. She questioned whether she would survive her pilgrimage. Her sufferings from thirst, particularly after she had gulped down brackish water because her camel driver could not communicate its danger, were almost unendurable. The wind blew fine sand into her face, burning and blinding her. The air shimmered above the heated earth. A mirage spread mocking waters and waving palms. Even the camels were quarrelsome and listless. She thought of the Israelites, with their women and children in this place, and was comforted!

She pored over the pages of Murray until it bored her. She turned to her Bible and 'was impressed afresh ... with its faithful localism.' She read with real experience phrases like 'rivers of water in a dry place' – 'a barren and thirsty land where no water is'. The scenery of the Wadi Shellal – the Valley of the Cataracts – called her back to life. She had thought the Rocky Mountains 'were all that nature could do in the way of colour' but she found 'the glorious peaks of the Sinaitic group far exceed them.' Her first view of Gebel Serbel was one of the most magnificent mountain views she ever saw. At last they reached water – the great oasis of Wadi Fairan. She drank rationally, as advised by her Arab companions, and they lifted her very gently from her camel and laid her on a blanket under a palm-tree.

Isabella was suffering from her existing illness and from dehydration, exhaustion and heat. Alexandre Dumas in 1837 had provided a very clear picture of what this means when he was in similar circumstances: 'I had suffered,' he wrote, 'the pains of a turtle boiled in his shell'; he feared he would fall from his camel; a hallucination seized him: his eyes were shut, but still he saw the sun, the sand and even the air; they had however changed their colour, and assumed strange tints. He imagined he was aboard a ship tossed by a troubled sea. He dreamed he fell from his camel, tried to run across the waves of sand and then to swim. Through his mind passed recollections of infancy, the murmur of a delightful brook in his father's garden. He was so confused he could not tell which of his impressions was the dream.[13]

That evening Isabella, after similar experiences, was sufficiently recovered to paint with words the scene as dusk drew in. Barley was springing up, flocks were nibbling herbage which, though scanty, was green; there was a murmur of water, and as she fell asleep that murmur became transformed into the sound of 'the river of the water of life' and the rustle of the palm fronds overhead into the whisper of the foliage of that tree 'whose leaves are for the healing of the nations.' Next morning, before the sun was fully risen, she was up and climbing to look at the ruins of Fairan – 'most mournful ruins in a solitary place'. From

---

[13] Alexandre Dumas, *Impressions de Voyage*, 194.

here, as she knew from her knowledge of the seventh century Antoninus Martyr, Moses viewed the battle of Rephidin.

She spent Easter Sunday in Wadi al-Shaikh, declaring it a day of rest during which she read the whole of the Old Testament from the twelfth chapter of Exodus (I think she means read the whole of Exodus from the twelfth chapter – it is still about fifty pages). This chapter gives God's commands to the Israelites that sent them out of Egypt and into the wilderness. Isabella read the Bible now as 'a new book, vivified, illuminated, intensified'.

As she and the shaikh rode up the Wadi Solap, she was still very ill. She lay in the shadow of a rock and looked up into 'the deep, pure, intense, delicious blue' sky that had taken over from the 'whitish, cruel, steely sky' of the desert. 'There was neither buzz nor hum of insect. The silence was absolute.' One catches in her words that feeling of disembodiment that attaches to illness. The evening of that day came at last 'with its coolness and tenderness' and 'in the midst of the transcendent beauty and grandeur' she saw ahead 'the fortress convent of St Catherine'.

This, like all else, far exceeded her expectations and was in complete harmony with its surroundings. She refused to stay within the convent and, after bickering and bargaining, pitched her tent on the hillside. The whole of the next day she gave over to reading and thinking, watching the mountain forms and 'revelling in her childish dream of a pilgrimage to Sinai, thus gloriously fulfilled.' Except for her servant and a single bee she saw not a living thing all day. She heard only the 'silver bells' of the cymbals of the monastic church and the call to prayer from the mosque in the convent (a mosque had been installed in the convent in 1106) and at night two hyenas that howled and prowled around. Later in the darkness a wind toppled her tent over and she spent the rest of the night, with a stone for a pillow, bitterly cold. She mentions this as a fact – uncomplainingly.

The sweet sound of the cymbals of the convent made her believe that the monks of St Catherine's were holy men, 'cultivating an exalted piety'. In this she was soon to be disenchanted. Inside the convent walls – which were no longer entered by a basket drawn up by a windlass as earlier travellers had experienced – she found, as we still do: '…a chaos of churches, chapels, mosques, minarets, storehouses, charnel-houses, galleries, distilleries, dormitories, rickety stair-cases, dark, low tunnels, roughly paved and very dirty open spaces, receptacles for rubbish, wells, some gone to ruin – all,' she concluded, 'in spite of the confusion, possessing a certain harmony and picturesqueness.'

The worship, as Harriet Martineau had explained, was solely that of the Greek Orthodox Church, although 'there was a time when many forms of religion were on an equality here.' Beside the great Greek church, the *muezzin* had once, within the walls of this Christian convent, called the Faithful to prayer. The Latins, Armenians and Syrians had also had chapels, but by 1847 as in Isabella's time, the Greek Orthodox was the only Christian sect in practice. An Orthodox service can seem strange – and very 'Eastern' – to those to whom it is unfamiliar. Isabella attended vespers in a very small chapel, and saw in the lengthy ritual the monks' apparent inattention and their 'howling of responses in coarse irreverent tones', with – to her – no realisation of the Divine presence. To her eyes, few of the monks' faces showed signs of holiness – the epithet 'villainous-looking' she found more appropriate. She was shocked too by the richness of the convent's trade and the way they taxed all traffic across the peninsula. She almost wished she had not visited the convent, so painful was the impression she brought away.

A monk guided her around the larger churches and she acknowledged their history and their splendour. The principal and magnificent Church of the Transfiguration astonished her with its architecture and wealth – hung with banners woven in silver and gold, and pendant gold and silver lamps gorgeously set with precious stones. She happily abandoned herself to the tradition that the Chapel of the Burning Bush (built by the Empress Helena in the fourth century) is the actual scene of God's revelation – and was inclined to take off her shoes to tread on the holy ground. In the library the monk burst forth into a vehement tirade against Constantin Tischendorf – as they did to us only a few years ago – because of the manuscript known as the Codex Sinaiticus which the Russian had 'borrowed' from the monastery and then sold to the Tsar, whose successors sold it to the British Museum; it lives in the British Library today.

In the convent gardens, Isabella contrasted the 'perennial greenness' to the arid, burning desert beyond its walls. Harriet Martineau was told that most of the soil was imported on camel back from the Nile's banks.[14] The monks were buried in the gardens, not far from the olive, the almond, the apples, the leeks, onions and lettuce, and the medicinal and sacred herbs which Miss Martineau had reported they sent out to the world. When their flesh had turned to dust, their remains went to the charnel-house where 'the holy and the unholy wait the resurrection trump together.' At its entrance sat St Stephen the Porter, arranged in gorgeous robes, his leathery, mummified face turned a little to one side with an expression of ghastly intelligence. Isabella toured through the grinning and leering skulls, the stacks of arms and hands and concluded, 'We do well to bury our dead out of sight.'

The next day before dawn she set off up Gebel Musa, at 7,375 feet established by sightings from the Red Sea the highest point of the Sinai ridge, and on to Ras Sufsafeh, the Mount of Law. Guided by a wizened bedu, even shorter than herself, at some points she had to be dragged up the great boulder steps by means of two straps. She passed through the arch where leathery Stephen the Porter had sat in life, and clambered to the peak.

She stayed there two hours – immersed in the Old Testament and the beauty. All the torments of the journey thither and the prospective misery of the journey

---

[14] Martineau, *op. cit.,* 311.

back had been worth these two contemplative hours to her. 'It was completely silent, unutterably lonely, awfully solemn.' She made her way along to the lonely, blasted summit of Ras Sufsafeh and sat all afternoon reading the last four books of Moses, and the conclusion of the Epistle of St Paul to the Hebrews XII. 'Wherefore, we receiving a kingdom which cannot be moved, let us have grace, whereby we may serve God acceptably with reverence and godly fear. For our God is a consuming fire.' Did Jehovah really speak to Moses here, she wondered? This was the sort of question that thousands of Christian and Muslim travellers have asked over the centuries. She lingered until late, struggling to remember and describe 'the complete carnival of colour' around her; words for the colours seemed hardly adequate. Orion wheeled majestically above – as it had when she sat with Rocky Mountain Jim high in the mountains more than ten years earlier. Before she left Sinai to suffer those 'prospective miseries', she sat and read by lamplight the end of the Epistle to the Hebrews: 'For our God is a consuming fire…' and felt she had seen it.

This journey for Isabella, more than any other before or later, was a real pilgrimage, carried out to a holy place at Easter. By early May she was on her way home. On board ship she sat up one night with an invalid passenger. It was this, she claimed, not the camel riding and the thirst and delirium, which brought on her agonising attack of pleurodynia which so weakened her that she could not for weeks walk from her house into the village of Tobermory on the island of Mull where she lived with her sister when she was not travelling. 'My body is very weak,' she wrote to a friend, 'but my head is all right, and I am working five hours a day in this delicious quiet.'

As ever, when something had to be done, whether it be writing a book or clambering to a mountain peak, Isabella Bird did it. But this pilgrimage she did not write about for six years and, curiously, her biographers ignored it, though they had the information to hand. Anna Stoddart, from whom other writers drew, knew when Isabella wrote up her notes for *The Leisure Hour* serial. This writing of her pilgrimage became linked to her husband's last days. He ailed – often given up for lost – for three long years. The diagnosis was pernicious anaemia – the treatment, sea air and a warm climate. In the late autumn of 1884 they travelled to the French Riviera. There Dr Bishop was confined to bed and she wrote to a friend in January 1885 that 'besides nursing him and reading to him' she did little but write 'two or three sheets of A Pilgrimage to Mount Sinai.' She had promised this to the editor of *The Leisure Hour*. She was not to finish it until the end of that year, in which the Bishops moved to Switzerland and, in November 1885, back to Cannes. The pilgrimage went off for publication and began to appear in its four parts just as Dr Bishop's days drew to a close.

Isabella's travels continued after Dr Bishop's death: in Kashmir and Tibet, Persia and Kurdistan, Korea, China and – in her seventieth year – a thousand-mile six-month tour of Morocco. She died in Edinburgh in October 1904 – her bags already packed for another journey to the East.

Bibliography

Barr, Pat, *A Curious Life for a Lady: The Story of Isabella Bird, traveller extraordinary* (London, 1970 and 1984).

Chubbuck, Kay, (ed.), *Letters to Henrietta* (London, 2002).

Hilmy, Ibrahim, *The Literature of Egypt and the Soudan from the earliest times to 1885: a bibliography* (London, 1886).

Kaye, Evelyn, *Amazing Traveler: Isabella Bird: The biography of a Victorian adventurer*, (USA, 1994) includes this pilgrimage.

The Leisure Hour, February–May, 1886.

Manning, Samuel, *Land of the Pharaohs: Egypt and Sinai – Illustrated with Pen and Pencil* (London, 1875).

Martineau, Harriet, *Eastern Life, Present and Past* (single volume edition) (Philadelphia, 1848).

Middleton, Dorothy (included Miss Bird in her) *Victorian Lady Travellers* (London, 1965).

Murray's *Handbook to Syria and Palestine* (London, 1875).

Stoddart, Anna M., *The Life of Isabella Bird* (1906).

Travelling Sketches of Egypt and Sinai, Including a Visit to Mount Horeb and Other Localities of the Exodus, translated from the French of Alexandre Dumas' *Impressions du Voyage,* by A Biblical Scholar (London, 1839).

Books by Isabella Bird

The Englishwoman in America (London, 1856).

Aspects of Religion in America (London, 1859).

Notes on Old Edinburgh (Edinburgh, 1869).

The Hawaiian Archipelago: Six months .. in the Sandwich Islands (London, 1875).

A Lady's Life in the Rocky Mountains (London, 1979).

Unbeaten Tracks in Japan (London, 1880).

The Golden Chersonese and the Way Thither (London, 1883).

Journeys in Persia and Kurdistan (London, 1891).

Among the Tibetans (London, 1894).

Korea and her Neighbours (London, 1898).

The Yangtze Valley and Beyond (London, 1899).

9. 'Women's Work for Women': American Presbyterian Missionary Women in Egypt, 1854–1914

Jeanne-Marie Warzeski

During the late nineteenth and early twentieth centuries, U.S. women made their way to Egypt as missionaries. Like the growing ranks of travellers making religious pilgrimages, young persons who enlisted for foreign missions responded in droves. Thousands of American men and women volunteered for mission service both at home and abroad, responding to what they believed to be the most pressing issue of their times: the evangelisation of the world. Fuelled by the doctrines of 'muscular Christianity', Social Gospel and millennarianism, missionaries became the natural successors to religious pilgrims in the Near East.

The sharp increase in American missionary activity during the last decades of the nineteenth century reflected an escalation of millennial thinking that occurred during the latter part of the century. Missionary zeal in the Near East arose from a similar ideological matrix as did Zionism: U.S. Christians and Jews alike sought to redeem Zion. Two otherwise disparate religious movements thus shared a crucial link.[1] Also, the Social Gospel preached by Rauschenbusch in the 1880s and 1890s to evangelise immigrants in American cities strongly influenced the missionary movement. Its followers held that the true Christian should address social programmes, including education, employment, health and living conditions.[2] The sense of social responsibility carried over to American interests overseas, where the perceived need was great for young Protestants to minister to 'heathens in Bible lands'. The term 'heathen' came to denote unevangelised communities, including Muslims, Roman Catholics in

---

[1] Henry Chadwick, 'Millennial History; Y2K—The Year 2000.'
[2] Jane Hunter, *The Gospel of Gentility*, 9.

'more benighted parts' (i.e., non-western countries) and 'nominal Christians' of the Middle East.[3]

As in England, the missionary movement in the United States was built on the idea that the propagation of 'civilising' Christianity would engender Western-style commerce and also bring about peace and happiness among its practitioners. The earliest U.S. efforts at evangelising the Middle East took place in 1818–19, when Pliny Fisk and Levi Parsons made an exploratory tour of the areas where the Seven Churches of Asia once stood. The American Board initially chose Damascus as its focus for missionary endeavor. By the 1850s, however, American Presbyterian missionary interests shifted to Egypt, and in 1854 two missionaries arrived in Cairo.

Logistics and politics bolstered the concept of an Egyptian mission, including inadequate opportunities in Damascus, the presumed favour of the Pasha, and the probability that distance from the Levant would provide insulation from the effects of the Eastern crisis (i.e., England, France, Austria-Hungary and Russia competed for power and influence in Turkey-in-Europe which slipped from Ottoman control, while the sultans continued to retain the allegiance of their Arab subjects in Turkey-in-Asia and the rest of the Empire). Indeed, Said Pasha did not discourage the nascent missionary enterprise, due in part to his penchant for western culture. Moreover, his administration fostered the development of communications and infrastructure which greatly facilitated missionary efforts: the 1850s saw the advent of steam and the institution of a telegraph system; the Cairo-Alexandria railway opened in 1856; and Ferdinand de Lesseps received a concession to build the Suez Canal in January 1856. These developments helped institutionalise the American missionary enterprise, reinforcing its administrative structure and reducing the isolation of the earlier days.

After 1858 the United Presbyterian Church of North America (UPCNA) directed the work of the Mission through the Board of Foreign Missions (BFM), a federation that held responsibility for all of the church's philanthropic works outside the U.S.[4] Noted mission pioneer Reverend Gulian Lansing opened a second mission station at Alexandria in 1857 and assumed responsibility for a girls' school that was formerly run by Scottish Presbyterians. In 1860 Lansing bought a Nile boat and travelled up the river distributing tracts. When a Syrian convert, Faris al-Hakim, was persecuted at Assiut in 1861, the American consul general intervened and imprisoned the persecutors. The Presbyterian Mission subsequently gained the respect of the Pasha, who presented the missionaries with a house in Cairo. The mission later purchased a facility in Alexandria.[5]

---

[3] See James K. Field, *America and the Mediterranean World*, 92–3.

[4] See Frederick J. Heuser, Jr., *Culture, Feminism and the Gospel: American Presbyterian Women and Foreign Missions, 1870–1923*, Chapter One.

[5] See Andrew Watson, *The American Mission in Egypt, 1854–1896*.

Single Lady Missionaries of the United Presbyterian Mission of North America. Photograph taken in Cairo, Egypt, about 1892 or 1893 (Abdullah Freres Photographs, Cairo, Egypt). Published courtesy of the Presbyterian Historical Society, Presbyterian Church U.S.A. (Philadelphia, PA).

The outburst of U.S. missionary activities in Egypt coincides with a growing 'feminine' interest in the Middle East. Operating within a background of millennial expectations and revivalist rhetoric, women who joined the foreign missionary movement were caught up in the spirit of the times and approached the field with youthful enthusiasm. Many wished to accomplish something useful and meaningful by devoting their lives to Christian values and service. The lives of two very different women, Henrietta Matilda McCague and Anna Young Thompson, exemplify the diverse goals, expectations and backgrounds that characterised female missionaries during the latter half of the nineteenth century.

Henrietta Matilda Lowes McCague entered the foreign mission field during the 1850s, a time when the Presbyterian Church, U.S.A. (then the Associate Reformed Presbyterian Church, or ARPC) made its initial efforts at mission work on a relatively limited scope. McCague and her husband, Rev. Thomas McCague, were appointed as missionaries to Egypt in 1854. Until their return to the U.S. in 1861, they taught and performed evangelistic work in Cairo and

Alexandria. The pattern of McCague's life in Egypt was similar to that of many U.S. women who volunteered for missionary service: that of teacher, evangelist, wife and mother.

The career of Anna Young Thompson spanned the years in which foreign mission work became transformed into a more global form of human outreach following the end of the U.S. Civil War. Thompson was appointed as a missionary to Egypt in 1871 under UPCNA. Until her retirement in 1931, she organised Sabbath schools, taught young girls and helped develop the first Christian Endeavor Society in Egypt. Thompson also organized the World Christian Temperance Union (WCTU) and served as its national president for many years.[6] Travellers and Egyptologists frequently referred to her work in mission schools in their journals.

Many women viewed missionary service as an alternative to the limited career options available to women and saw missionary work as an opportunity to achieve professional satisfaction. Mission literature offered models for the 'new Christian woman professional' that challenged the Victorian model (and Pauline stereotype) of womanhood, emphasising qualities such as courage, leadership and industry. Mission work enabled many women to gain a sense of autonomy with less gender discrimination than otherwise possible in nineteenth century United States. Still others sought adventure and the opportunity to experience another culture.

Frederick Heuser compares the zeal that women had for the cause of foreign missions to a crusade. The mission field may have provided escape from an uncomfortable or meaningless situation at home. Yet, during the nineteenth century, the turnover rate in foreign missionary work was quite high. Many vacancies occurred among the Presbyterian female mission force due to illness, deaths and resignations.[7] Service in Africa and the Middle East in particular involved greater risk of death in the field than in other mission areas. Causes of death included accidents, acts of violence due to local or general wartime conflict and the occasional suicide.

Possibly the single greatest motivating factor for many women to the field was the belief that indigenous peoples could be spiritually, socially and intellectually transformed. This concept stems from the evangelical tradition that upholds that with the help of God an individual is innately capable of altering his or her spiritual condition. As early as the 1780s, evangelical enthusiasm had inspired a barrage of debates on the question of 'civilizing and

---

[6] Anna Young Thompson's life is the subject of a hagiography by a fellow missionary: Elizabeth Kelsey Kinnear, *She Sat Where They Sat; A Memoir of Anna Young Thompson of Egypt.*

[7] Heuser, *op. cit.,* 58.

improving' non-European peoples.[8] The development of trade in non-European areas seemed morally to legitimise western intervention in Africa, the Middle East and Asia.[9] Young Presbyterians during the latter half of the nineteenth century consequently responded to what they felt to be the most pressing issue of their times: the evangelisation of the world.

For many women, the call to mission work reflected a genuine desire to do something useful and meaningful with their lives. Missionary service offered middle-class women an opportunity to influence the lives of indigenous women and the means to redefine themselves in this context. Women who served overseas and the thousands of female supporters of missionary societies at home directed their efforts to the plight of foreign women. Candidates for the mission field viewed women in far-flung 'exotic' locales as victims of child marriages, illiteracy and aberrant cultural practices. Denominational leaders could cite accounts of practices that were offensive to Western notions of family and individual dignity, such as of footbinding (China), polygamy (the Middle East), or *sati* (India), to underline the need for foreign missions. Such literature contrasted the enlightened position of Western Christian women with their 'benighted sisters' in non-Christian lands that were victimised by 'heathen customs'. As Frederick J. Heuser emphasizes, such literature demonstrated the denomination's belief that men and women bore equal responsibility for the evangelisation of the East.[10]

Many missionaries were overly confident in their initial commitment to the cause but were ill prepared to deal with the reality of life in Egypt. Their views of the East were informed by inaccurate and condescending caricatures conveyed in denominational literature. Mission periodicals, such as the popular *Women's Work for Women*, openly criticised unfamiliar cultural practices and promulgated an image of Egypt as an economically, culturally and morally impoverished nation in need of Christian salvation. Stories from furloughed missionaries similarly conveyed little of substance about life in the mission field. By the end of the century, however, this narrowness was tempered by a growing sensitivity to indigenous cultural institutions, including religion. In fact, later editions of mission periodicals showed that it was difficult (if not impossible and in fact

---

[8] See J.M. Warzeski, 'Evangelicalism and Imperialism: The Sierra Leone and Botany Bay Schemes,' 15–17.

[9] See William R. Hutchinson, 'Modernism and Missions: The Liberal Search for an Exportable Christianity, 1875–1935,' in John K. Fairbank, *The Missionary Enterprise in China and America*, 110–131; Thomas Prasch, 'Which God for Africa: The Islamic-Christian Missionary Debate in Late-Victorian England,' 51–74; Andrew Porter, 'Commerce and Christianity: The Rise and Fall of a Nineteenth-Century Missionary Slogan,' 597–621.

[10] Heuser, *op. cit.*, 14.

undesirable) to transform indigenous cultures in a Western image.[11]

By contemporary Egyptian criteria, the standard of living for missionaries was high. They lived in large houses, employed numerous servants and ate well. They owned horses and donkeys for transport and travelled extensively within the country as well as in Europe on their way to and from the U.S. Yet by Western standards their lives would have been considered difficult and lacking in many ordinary comforts. Many underestimated the circumstances they were to encounter because their initial days in the field gave them an incomplete knowledge of the actual conditions they were to encounter.

Because of the high expectations generated by mission propaganda, many missionaries experienced considerable feelings of self-doubt and anxiety. Upon her arrival in Egypt in 1871, 21-year-old Anna Young Thompson expressed her eagerness to explore the country but felt uncertain she had the qualifications 'to labor in the Lord's vineyard'. Moreover she feared dying in Egypt and contracting ophthalmia.[12] Incidentally, Thompson's dread of ophthalmia was well founded, as Egypt was notorious as a place where both foreigner and Egyptian alike contracted an eye infection that often left its sufferers blind. Henrietta Matilda McCague suffered from the affliction twice, as did her husband and two children who were born during their tenure in Egypt. She described the condition: 'Your eye feels as though it were a burning ball of lead in the socket and the scalding hot tears run down your cheeks and the least degree of light is almost unsupportable. (…).'[13] Other hardships included cholera and other epidemics. The McCagues described the devastating impact of the 1855 cholera epidemic and feared for their lives.[14] They lost their son, James Irwin (b. Dec. 10, 1855) to smallpox in April 1857. Their remaining son, Johnnie, was constantly ill.

For the McCagues, as for others, life in Egypt must have seemed insufferable at times. Moreover, women with an evangelical background found it difficult to separate a spiritual from a non-spiritual crisis. Factors precipitating a crisis included feelings of self-doubt about the state of the soul or the content of one's character, which in turn produced guilt that manifested in a variety of physical and emotional symptoms (e.g., nerves, fainting, and depression). Since denominational literature made heroes out of past missionaries and overdramatised their attributes and accomplishments, many new recruits felt inadequate to the call.

After years of living overseas, 'successful' young missionaries often

---

[11] *Ibid.,* 223–4.

[12] *Anna Young Thompson Papers,* (58-1-9), diary entry, Dec. 7, 1871 (Cairo).

[13] *McCague Family Papers* MS M113t (30), Mrs. (Henrietta Matilda Lowes) McCague to her brother and sister-in-law, Oct. 13, 1856.

[14] *McCague Family Papers,* MS M113t (23), Rev. Thomas McCague to Parents and Brothers at Home, June 15, 1855.

experienced a kind of transformation in which they identified more with the adopted country than with their own.[15] Such a reversal in identification required their ultimate acceptance of indigenous people and their culture, rather than the uninformed view that non-Western cultures had to be changed to fit the mission ideal. Yet the degree to which missionary women became acculturated varied considerably. Those who spent their entire careers in Egypt, such as Anna Young Thompson, became more immersed in the indigenous culture than those who used their stint as missionaries as stepping stones to something else. Most young missionaries initially failed to understand the process of cultural change. Indeed, even the most broadly tolerant among them found it initially difficult to accept non-Western cultures and practices in a non-judgmental way. For example, when Anna Young Thompson first attended a Coptic liturgy, she was unable to keep from laughing, due to the distracting crowds of people and animals that found their way into the church.

Female missionaries' initial perceptions of Egyptian customs were un-informed and naïve. Like other young missionaries of their generation, they held to the erroneous assumption that the non-Protestant world was 'a monolithic mass that could be manipulated and liberated with scriptural injunctions and American gunboats.'[16] The 'heathen woman', oppressed by child marriage, polygamy, and illiteracy, became a potent symbol of this notion. Henrietta McCague described the life of *fellahin* women as arduous, consisting of preparing their husbands' food, transporting water in large earthen jars on their heads, spinning, and making fuel to heat their ovens from the dung of cattle that was picked up in the streets and fields and carried home in baskets on their heads, mixed with chopped straw and then moulded into flat round cakes and stuck on the walls and roofs of their houses to dry in the sun. She concluded that 'women contribute more than their husbands to the support of their families yet they are not always permitted to sit with their husbands and when they go out with their lords they generally walk behind them and carry the bundle if there is one to be carried.'[17]

Other mission women similarly described Egyptian women as leading lives of drudgery. Most became sympathetic to the problems of poor women. However, many failed to see the real causes of these problems, such as the lack of clean water or medical help, and in their official writings attributed them solely to ignorance or immorality. In a letter to the Muskingum Ohio Women's Missionary Society, Anna Young Thompson demonstrated sympathy for Coptic

---

[15] Heuser, 'Women's Work for Women: Belle Sherwood Hawkes and the East Persia Presbyterian Mission,' 16.

[16] Heuser, *Culture, Feminism and the Gospel*, 29.

[17] *McCague Family Papers,* MS M113t (29), Mrs. (Henrietta Matilda Lowes) McCague to her cousin Eliza, Mar. 15, 1856.

and Muslim women, and attributed Egyptian women's lack of 'improvement' to ignorance.[18] 'Women's Work for Women' – evangelism, education and medical programmes aimed at indigenous women – thus became the province of female Presbyterians both at home and in the field to liberate women from their perceived cultural oppression and spiritual impoverishment. The hope was that Egyptian women would in turn nurture a 'Christian character' within their families and communities. This moralistic approach to society's ills also resonated in a vast literature describing the conditions of the working classes, both in Great Britain and the United States, during the nineteenth century.

As homemakers, teachers or evangelists (and later as doctors and nurses), mission women took on a role of parental authority for Egyptian women and girls, who in turn took in every detail of the conduct, speech, dress and mannerisms of their mentors. Acutely aware of their status as role models, female missionaries espoused the belief that character formation was nurtured through maternal influence. A married missionary woman served as a model homemaker to demonstrate that she and her husband practised what they preached. Both single and married women saw themselves in familial terms, as a 'mother' or an elder sister, an identification they carried into all their activities, whether it was teaching, nursing, visiting friends and neighbours, or reading scripture.

The U.S. Presbyterian church sent 'harem workers' to visit and instruct thousands of women in their homes. Known to as *zenana*, this type of house-to-house calling permitted western women entrance into the homes of Middle Eastern women, where they could read Scripture as well as attend to basic needs. *Zenana*, a Hindi term, refers to the part of the house in India or Pakistan reserved for the women of the household. The Presbyterian missionary endeavour commenced in India in 1852, a year before efforts were made in Egypt and Syria. Apparently, Presbyterian missionaries borrowed the Hindi term to refer to women's ministering to women and children in the harem throughout the Middle East.

House visits permitted an intensive one-to-one exchange, similar to visitations conducted by social workers, which allowed both missionary and Egyptian woman to come to a better understanding about each other's culture.[19] Anna Young Thompson visited as many as fifteen homes a day. These visits helped to break down mutual prejudices and create bonds with Egyptian women. Yet, the success rate, measured in terms of conversions, remained astonishingly low in Egypt. One traveller noted during the 1890s, "Though their wish and aim from

---

[18] *Anna Young Thompson Papers,* (58-1-4), AYT to Muskingum W.M.S., 3 May 1888 (Cairo).

[19] Michael P. Zirinsky, 'Harbingers of Change: Presbyterian Women in Iran, 1883–1949,' 175.

the first has been a missionary one to proselites [sic], they confessed to us at the American College at Assiout when we were here before, that they were never successful, as a Muslim changed into a Christian is almost unknown."[20] Missionaries therefore concentrated on the Coptic population, which they regarded as "nominal Christians" and living in squalor.

Itineration, the rural counterpart of *zenana*, consisted of evangelical tours into the hinterland where few white women had ever ventured. These preaching tours, usually considered the province of male missionaries, provided a more comprehensive sense of Egyptian conditions. As areas became more accessible, women also began to undertake these sojourns. They were usually eye-opening experiences for both missionaries and indigenous women.

The women's boards and the Board of Foreign Missions came to support a system of primary and secondary schools that provided a curriculum of religious instruction and academic subjects. Two types of mission-supported institutions emerged during the 1850s–60s: those that served Muslims and those that served the indigenous Christian community. Schools for Muslims, known as day schools, provided basic elementary education for girls from needy families. The objective was to convert Muslim parents through their children, in whom the missionaries hoped to develop a "Christian character" through religious instruction and the promotion of Western hygiene standards. Mission boarding schools, on the other hand, attended by children of native Christians, missionaries, diplomats and businessmen, offered a more diverse curriculum, including history, physiology, natural history, and music.[21] Mission schools were recognised for their superior curriculum and teaching and became a showpiece in Cooks' tours and other package tours of Egypt to demonstrate the efficacy of Western-run institutions. Consequently, many wealthy grand tourists and Egyptologists sponsored young Egyptian girls as pupils at mission-run schools.

The establishment of educational institutions for girls challenged the existing social structure and often met with strong resistance. Missionaries often bemoaned the fact that the society did not value the education of girls. In July 1855, Henrietta Matilda McCague observed that "there are a number of schools here for boys and many of them are taught to read and write, but there is but one for girls among the natives" and concluded that "Girls are not loved as well as boys, and their parents think that it is not necessary for them to learn to read."[22] Anna Young Thompson also remarked on the apparent preference toward boys in Egyptian families. She wrote:

---

[20] Mrs. Emma B. Andrews, *A Journal on the Bedawin 1889-1912,* entry for 7 February 1893 (Assouan), II, 73.

[21] Heuser, *Culture, Feminism and the Gospel,* 167.

[22] *McCague Family Papers,* MS M113t (25), Mrs. (Henrietta Matilda Lowes) McCague to a Sunday school class in Ohio, ca. July, 1855,

Several girls in a family are considered a calamity, and sometimes the father is so angry over the birth of a daughter he will not speak to the mother or look at the child for days, and all the friends have sorrowful faces. But there is always rejoicing over a boy. I have often asked why girls are not welcome and the answer is sometimes "They are only an expense and bring in nothing to the family," but nearly always the answer is "The girls marry young and leave us, but the boys remain at home with us" even when married, unless business calls them to move elsewhere.[23]

Thompson's remarks show an informed understanding of Egyptian family life that reflected her longer tenure in Egypt.

In some respects, missionary efforts to improve the condition of indigenous women paralleled the goals of the broader women's movement. U.S. feminist Charlotte Beebe Wilbour, wife of Egyptologist Charles Edwin Wilbour, had ample opportunity to observe Egyptian women firsthand during her many years of travel during the 1880s. In 1887 she delivered an address to the Association for the Advancement of Women in which she spoke her experiences while travelling down the Nile with her family aboard their floating research vessel, *The Seven Hathors*.[24] She observed that the condition of women and children had became 'yet more hopelessly degraded' due to the severe taxation and forced military conscription of the local farmers, the *fellahin*.[25] As did missionary women, Mrs. Wilbour primarily attributed women's degraded position to early marriages, divorce and concubinage, conditions which she saw as sanctioned by Islam. Moreover, she wrote that 'wherever there has been a reduction of public or charitable appropriations, the needed economy has at once been applied to the women's share; many schools for girls have been closed to eke out the scrimped allowance for the boys.'[26] In this context she praised American mission schools for their efforts to ameliorate female illiteracy in Egypt.

Mrs. Wilbour's programme appears astonishingly similar to that of American missionary women. In fact, some scholars maintain that women missionaries became symbols of potential self-realisation for indigenous women.[27] They saw their power as the influence they could exert within their separate sphere as women. Like those who crusaded for temperance, female missionaries rejected the call for political rights; instead, they saw evangelism and social service programs as the means to effect change. Unwittingly, perhaps, they comm-unicated dignity and self-respect for millions of indigenous women but it was in

---

[23] *Anna Young Thompson Papers,* (58-1-4), 'A Pen Picture of Egyptian Children' (n.d., 1872-1906).

[24] Charlotte Beebe Wilbour, *Of Egyptian Women; Address delivered to the Fifteenth Annual Congress of the Association for the Advancement of Women, New York, 1887*, 6.

[25] *Ibid.*

[26] *Ibid.*

[27] Heuser, *Culture, Feminism and the Gospel*, 250.

the context of a Christian programme rather than through a consciously feminist agenda.[28] One must therefore caution against conflating missionary efforts with incipient feminism. Missionary women did not support female suffrage or political revolution as legitimate causes to improve the condition of women. In fact, many believed that the quest for suffrage and equal rights would neither improve the condition of indigenous women nor enhance their own status within the denomination. Anna Young Thompson noted that '[a] plurality of wives is slowly going out of fashion among the educated and higher classes, but there is perhaps not always a higher state of morals.'[29] Instead, missionary women saw western Christianity as the vehicle that would ultimately free indigenous women from the superstitions and negative behaviour that they perceived as endemic to local culture.

In their belief that social problems could be resolved through spiritual transformation, missionaries were idealists. They embraced the belief that indigenous women had the power to control their destinies, a concept supported by the evangelical ethic. They maintained that women should be free to make their own decisions about their lives, whether it was the clothing they wore or what career they should have. Missionary women thus provided a model of what women could become. However, the model they offered as an alternative was hardly one of female liberation: it was that of Victorian domestic ideology which effectively embraced as much sequestration of women (in an ideological sense) as did the harem.

Margaret Strobel maintains that western women became actively engaged in the cultural aspects of imperialism through their gender roles as caretakers and 'civilizers.'[30] Missionary women contributed to colonial appropriation because they saw themselves as assisting in the redemption of the Muslim world and 'enlightening' Egyptian women through their exemplification of Western gender roles. Yet to write off the foreign missionary movement as merely a subset of imperialism would be to trivialise the accomplishments of those individuals who did, in fact, achieve a broader understanding of Egyptian culture. Of all travellers to Egypt, those who participated in missions were in the best position to convey a much deeper understanding of Middle Eastern women, because the nature of their work demanded that they come to accept a host culture on its own terms. For those who devoted their lives to the cause, the mission field was a place where East did indeed meet West. Successful missionaries did not change Egyptian culture through conversions to Presbyterianism but through what Yahya Armajani calls the application of the

---

[28] Heuser, 'Women's Work for Women,' 16.
[29] Anna Young Thompson, 'Reform in Egypt,' in A. van Sommer and S.M. Zwemmer (eds.). *Daylight in the Harem; A New Era for Moslem Women* (1911), 110.
[30] See Margaret Strobel, *European Women and the Second British Empire*.

'evangelical ethic': they realised the impossibility of changing the country through conversion but focused instead on influencing future generations through education and the introduction of new values.[31] The world envisioned by the idealists of the 1890s ultimately may not have come to pass. But there is no doubt that these pioneers made an impact and irrevocably altered the future for Egyptian women in terms of increased educational opportunities and legal rights, causes that the indigenous feminist movement took up during the twentieth century.

Bibliography

Andrews, Emma B., *A Journal on the Bedawin 1889–1912. The Diary kept on board the dahabiyeh of Theodore M. Davis during seventeen trips up the Nile by Mrs. Emma B. Andrews.* Unpublished typescript, Metropolitan Museum of Art, New York.

Chadwick, Henry, 'Millennial History; Y2K—The Year 2000,' National Public Radio, *To the Best of Our Knowledge,* 16 August 1998.

Fairbank, John K., *The Missionary Enterprise in China and America.* Cambridge, Cambridge University Press, 1974.

Field, James K., *America and the Mediterranean World.* Princeton, New Jersey, Princeton University Press, 1969.

Heuser, Frederick J., Jr. 'Women's Work for Women: Belle Sherwood Hawkes and the East Persian Presbyterian Mission,' *American Presbyterians: Journal of Presbyterian History* 65, 1 (Spring 1987).

Heuser, Jr., Frederick J., *Culture, Feminism and the Gospel: American Presbyterian Women and Foreign Missions, 1870–1923.* Ph.D. Thesis, Temple University, Philadelphia, Pennsylvania, 1991.

Hunter, Jane, *The Gospel of Gentility; American Women Missionaries in Turn-of-the-Century China.* New Haven, Connecticut, Yale University Press, 1984.

Kinnear, Elizabeth Kelsey, *She Sat Where They Sat; A Memoir of Anna Young Thompson of Egypt.* Grand Rapids, Michigan, Christian World Mission Books, William B. Erdmans Publishing Co., 1971.

McCague, Henrietta Matilda Lowes, *McCague Family Papers, 1855–56.* Philadelphia, Pennsylvania, The Department of History, Presbyterian Church (U.S.A.), Board of Foreign Missions, Egypt Mission (Associate Reformed Church),

Miller, Robert J. (ed), *Religious Ferment in Asia.* Lawrence, Kansas, University of Kansas Press, 1974.

Porter, Andrew, 'Commerce and Christianity': The Rise and Fall of a Nineteenth-Century Missionary Slogan," *Historical Journal* 28 (1985), 597–621.

Prasch, Thomas, 'Which God for Africa: The Islamic-Christian Missionary Debate in Late-Victorian England,' *Victorian Studies* 33,1 (1989), 51–74

---

[31] Yahya Armajani, "Sam Jordan and the Evangelical Ethic in Iran," in Robert J. Miller, ed., *Religious Ferment in Asia,* 22–36.

Strobel, Margaret, *European Women and the Second British Empire.* Bloomington, Indiana, Indiana University Press, 1991.

Thompson, Anna Young, *Diary and Correspondence, 1871–1906.* Philadelphia, Pennsylvania: The Department of History, Presbyterian Church (U.S.A.), Board of Foreign Missions, Egypt Mission (Associate Reformed Church),

Van Sommer, A. and S.M. Zwemmer (eds.), *Daylight in the Harem; A New Era for Moslem Women. Papers on Present-Day Reform Movements, Conditions and Methods of Work among Moslem Women. Second Missionary Conference on Behalf of the Mohommedan World, Lucknow, 1911.* Edinburgh/London, Oliphant, Anderson and Ferrier, 1911.

Warzeski, J.M., 'Evangelicalism and Imperialism: The Sierra Leone and Botany Bay Schemes,' *Raconteur* (Tallahassee, Florida), 1, 1 (Summer 1990): 9–25.

Watson, Andrew, *The American Mission in Egypt, 1854–1896.* Pittsburgh, Pennsylvania, United Presbyterian Board of Publication, 1904.

Wilbour, Charlotte Beebe, *Of Egyptian Women; Address delivered to the Fifteenth Annual Congress of the Association for the Advancement of Women, New York, 1887.* Paris, France: Privately Printed, 1887.

Zirinsky, Michael P., "Harbingers of Change: Presbyterian Women in Iran, 1883–1949," *American Presbyterians* 70:3 (1992), 173–86.

10. Perceptions of Women in the Eastern Desert of Egypt

Janet Starkey

Orientalism, in which fact and fantasy are intertwined, has strongly influenced the ways in which the women of the Middle East have been viewed. A western and male construct, Orientalism has treated Oriental women as objects both of knowledge and also of desire. As Said himself wrote 'The Orient was Orientalized not only because it was discovered to be "Oriental" in all those ways considered commonplace by an average nineteenth-century European, but also because it *could be* [...] *made* "Oriental"',[1] through the strength of colonialism.[2]

These ideas can be tested against the travel writers' descriptions of the women from Beja tribes who inhabit the Eastern Desert of Egypt. Most writers on the women of Egypt, such as Judith E. Tucker[3] and Karin van Nieuwkerk,[4] almost exclusively confine their accounts to Lower Egypt and the Cairenes. These were the communities in Egypt that were affected most by European colonialism, with all its economic and political ramifications, unlike the peoples of the Eastern Desert who remained largely outside the colonialist sphere of influence.

The major tribe of the Eastern Desert is the Beja. Its principal sub-groups are the 'Ababda, Amarar, Bisharin, and Hadendoa. In Eritrea and around Kassala in Sudan live other Beja groups. There may be as many as 58,000 'Ababda and Bisharin Beja speakers and 142,000 'Ababda Arabic speakers, with about 41,155 Bisharin in Sudan today. The 'Ababda are scattered over the Nubian Desert and

---

[1] *Orientalism* (London, Routledge and Kegan Paul, 1978), 5–6.

[2] Meyda Yeğenoğlu, *Colonial Fantasies: towards a feminist reading of Orientalism* (Cambridge, Cambridge University Press, 1998), 17.

[3] *Women in Nineteenth-Century Egypt* (Cambridge, Cambridge University Press, 1985).

[4] *'A Trade like any Other': female singers and dancers in Egypt* (Austin, University of Texas Press, 1995).

in the Nile Valley with the greater part of the tribe living around Daraw where they control the camel market, trading in the major clearing house of Aswan, and in the northern part of the Atbai. The Ma'aza, a Beduin tribe which migrated from Arabia, with whom they do not intermarry, roam the Eastern Desert north of the 'Ababda, the desert route from the Nile to the Red Sea from Qina to al-Qusayr forming the boundary between them. The Bisharin are scattered over the Batn al-Hajar (Nubian Desert) and in the Nile valley where they have settled in their own villages and practice agriculture: for them Jabal Elba near the Red Sea coast is a sacred mountain.[5]

It is surprising how few modern scholars recall the Eastern Desert and its Beja tribes from travel literature on Egypt, let alone anything about their women. Deserts have been idealised and have become exotic places in an imaginary Orient: travel into the desert was tinged with romance. However, many of the travellers' accounts of the desert and the women who went or were found there are far from romantic and are relatively free from metaphorical allusions. The accounts are often intimate and realistic, full of ethnographically authentic information, full of the harsh realities of life. Writers approach their experiences from many angles: some admire the local people, others fear them, whilst most learn to understand them as neighbours. What does emerge from a range of travel literature is an apparently authentic picture, albeit hazy, of women in the Eastern Desert.

To be fair, few travellers ever ventured into the region. If they crossed the desert, they had to endure many hardships, intense heat, poor and intermittent water supplies, violent sandstorms and hunger. The 'Ababda lived essentially outside the framework of the colonialist umbrella, so does this, in some way, mean that they are alien to the Orientalist idiom? In fact, far from living in splendid isolation in the mountains and valleys of the Eastern Desert unfrequented by travellers, the Beja tribes were occupied on the main trade routes between the Nile valley and the Red Sea, transporting all the luxury goods required to support the Nilotic states. 'Ababda men provided and protected the pilgrim routes and corn caravans, especially between Qina on the Nile to al-Qusayr on the Red Sea coast, a journey that took four to five days by camel or ten hours by car. They also controlled the route across the Nubian Desert from Daraw via Korosko to Abu Hamed in Nubia.

Western Women in the Eastern Desert

British ships *en route* to or from India called at al-Qusayr until the 1830s, with numerous Europeans travelling across the desert to visit the antiquities on the Nile, such as Mrs. Katherine Elwood in 1825. She describes the scenery:

---

[5] Janet Starkey, 'Perceptions of the Ababda and Bisharin in the Atbai', *Sudan Studies* 26 (2001) (http://www.sssuk.org).

It is not easy to conceive the sterile grandeur of the scene, and the singularity of our position, encamped in the heart of the Desert, surrounded by wild Arabs, every moment liable to an attack from some wandering tribe, and totally dependent upon the good faith of our Abadè guide for safety. [...] Certainly, no fine lady, who could not do without her everyday luxuries and comforts, should attempt the Desert of the Thebaid [...] I infinitely preferred this patriarchal style of life, free and unshackled as it was, to the artificial stupidity of civilisation.

She found 'the serenity of the scene, the purity of the air, the exquisite beauty of the stars, all contributed their *agreements*.'[6]

By the 1840s, European women still occasionally crossed the Eastern Desert, despite the development of the Overland Route between Alexandria and Suez. In 1847, Sir J. G. Wilkinson, gave them the following advice:

a lady [should] bring a side-saddle for a donkey, and panniers for children; and if not in too great a hurry, the desert can be crossed without inconvenience or fatigue. But a lady ought not to do it in less than seven days, which should be told to the camel owners before leaving Ḵossayr, that they may take sufficient means etc for themselves and camels; if not they will make it an excuse to push on.[7]

Not all descriptions of the region were unsympathetic. Although the opening of Suez Canal in 1869 extinguished the Eastern Desert as an east-west route between the Nile and the Red Sea, the 'Ababda continued to provide camels for tourist trips, for customs officials and for those policing the desert. For example, Edward North Buxton and his daughters, Hannah Maud, Clare Emily and Theresa Buxton, explored the Eastern Desert in February 1893 to secure specimens of the Arabic or Sinaitic ibex.[8] The daughters published their experiences in *On Either Side of the Red Sea* (1895) and illustrated the volume with photographs they took with an ordinary Kodak camera which were reprinted by the Swan Electric Engraving Company. Although they do not shed many of their western perceptions in the short period of their expedition, they present an enjoyable and empathetic picture of desert life. They travelled in style, taking turkeys, sheep and chickens with them. They 'were allowed a pint and a half [of water] for the evening wash, and this had to be carefully treasured up till the next morning!'[9]

---

[6] Mrs. Catherine [Anne Katherine] Elwood, *Narrative of a Journey Overland by the Continent of Europe, Egypt and the Red Sea to India, including a Residence there and a voyage home, 1825–1828* (London, H. Colburn and R. Bentley 1830).

[7] *Handbook for Travellers in Egypt* (London, John Murray, 1847; 1896), 400.

[8] *Capra beden.* It is a wild goat called *wa'l* by Arabs outside the area and *badan* by local Arab tribesmen, see Bible Master website at http://www.biblemaster.com/bible/ency/isb/view.asp?number=3841 for further details.

[9] Buxton, 57.

Their first night was spent at Bir Arras, fourteen miles from Qina, in an elaborate camp: 'it was very exciting watching the tents being put up, and our camp looks so comfortable. [...] We have just been dining outside, in the delicious crisp air. It was pitch dark, but the camp was lighted by Chinese lanterns. The dinner which our old black cook produced was beyond expectation.'[10] By the time they reached Wadi Medisa, they found it easier to camp out in the moonlight: 'We came to the conclusion that tents are superfluous luxuries in this climate. At least this *al fresco* camp was the one we liked best, and, by sharing our meals and our fire with our Bedawin, we got on more friendly terms with them.'

They met both Ma'aza and 'Ababda on their travels. 'We found the Maazeh tribe of Bedawin very considerate towards ladies, and solicitous for their comfort, It is unlikely that this Arab had ever seen European ladies before, and their independence somewhat alarmed him' (p. 79). 'The ['Ababda] tribe use tents, or rather huts, of mats made of plaited palm leaves – a sign, I think, of the scantiness of their flocks' (p. 91). They camped in Umm Anab on March 3rd 1893 and found 'a little settlement of Ababdeh Arabs [...] The women and children especially were shy, and hastily retired to their tents, where they sat with their backs to us. We tried to propitiate them with chocolates, which the children were only too ready for, but their mammas promptly threw them away' (pp. 83–85). They reached Qina on 11 March 1893, 'when at last the palm trees of Keneh came in sight [...] they all began singing and shouting at the tops of their voices.' (p. 92). Such tourist treks became increasingly infrequent and by 1900 the country between Wadi 'Araba and the Qina-al-Qusayr road was essentially uninhabited.

On the Women of the Eastern Desert

These nineteenth-century European women's accounts are interesting from a western perspective but tell us little about the women of the area, except that they went on pilgrimages, were sympathetic to strangers and generally had a hard life. It is in the writings of male travellers in the area that we begin to get a clearer picture of the individual character of women in the region.

Strange snippets about the people of the area reach us from Classical times. Diodorus Siculus[11] quoted Agatharchides of Cnidus, tutor of Ptolemy X (c.170–120 BC) and wrote of a pastoral tribe and the lax morality of its women. 'The Kings of Egypt condemn vast multitudes to the mines [...] whole families are doomed to this labour, with a view to punishing the guilty and profiting by their toil.' Of the Ichthyophagi, 'They go naked [...] and have their wives in common,

---

[10] *Ibid.*, 51–2.

[11] *Bibliothicae historicae libri qui supersunt. Interprete Laurentio Rhodomano, recensuit Petrus Wesseingius* (Amsterdam, 1746), quoted in A. Paul, *History of the Beja Tribes of the Sudan* (1954; repr. London, Frank Cass, 1971), 34.

[…] and like other fish-eating people they do not drink. They live in caves, tents of grass, under trees, or in holes dug in the sea moss.'[12]

A search of the texts of medieval Arab writers provides a few insights into the life of the Red Sea area. Apart from references to the inhospitable environment and dangerous coastline, they mentioned Beja nomads who hired out camels and guides but were likely to steal travellers' possessions, plunder their ships or leave them to die in the desert. The Red Sea ports of 'Aydhab and Suakin were flourishing despite their uninviting inhabitants; their trade was based on pepper and other spices, Chinese porcelain, ivory, pearls, precious metals and textiles and other exotic goods from the Mediterranean, Africa, Nubia and Asia as well as the transport of thousands of Muslim pilgrims *en route* to and from Mecca.

Further comments on women of the area were provided by medieval Arab writers. The Andalusian traveller and pilgrim, Abu'l-Husayn Muhammad ibn Ahmad ibn Jubayr (b.1145), spent eight months in Mecca and as part of his account of his travels to make the *hajj*, returning to Spain in April 1185. In his *Rihla* he described his journey from Qus on the Nile in May–July 1183. He wrote about the perils of the waterless desert and the dangers of coral reefs in the Red Sea, as well as the ill-treatment of pilgrims, presumably both men and women, *en route* from the Nile via 'Aydhab and the Red Sea to Jiddah. Having stayed in 'Aydhab for twenty-three days, he claimed that its inhabitants had no religion 'save the formal words … to display that they are Muslims. But behind that are corrupt beliefs and practices that cannot be condoned and are unlawful.' He described the people of 'Aydhab as belonging to a Sudanese tribe called al-Bujat: 'their men and women go naked abroad, wearing nothing but the rag which covers their genitals, and most not even this. In a word they are a breed of no regard and it is no sin to pour maledictions upon them.'[13] Al-Tugaibi, travelling between Qus and 'Aydhab around 1271 provides a similar account of the people of 'Aydhab: 'The harbour is excellent. The people, men and women, go about naked except for a tiny piece of cloth or skin covering their private parts. Women's hair is exposed and so are their breasts. It is to be mentioned that they do not punish for adultery nor feel ashamed of it.'[14]

Probably the greatest traveller of medieval Arab world was Abu 'Abdallah ibn Battuta who was born in Tangier in 1304[15] and described his adventures in

---

[12] *Letters,* III, 15.

[13] R. J. C. Broadhurst, *The Travels of Ibn Jubayr* (London, Jonathan Cape, 1952), 59–68 (66).

[14] Al-Turaibi, *Mustafad al-rihla wa-al-ightirab,* ed. 'Abd al-Hafiz Mansur (Libya, 1975), 206, quoted in 'Okasha El-Daly, 'Early Medieval Arab Travel Writings', in *Desert Travellers from Herodotus to T. E. Lawrence* ed. Janet Starkey and Okasha El Daly (Durham, ASTENE, 2000), 30.

[15] Ross E. Dunn, *The Adventures of Ibn Battuta* (Berkeley, Ca., University of California Press, 1986), 53–4.

his *Rihla*. In 1326 he planned to travel to Mecca from Egypt on his own, not with the official Egyptian pilgrimage caravan that travelled by Sinai, but by the commercial route for spices via Upper Egypt and across the Red Sea hills to 'Aydhab to catch a boat to Jiddah. He described 'Aydhab as 'a large town, well supplied with milk and fish; dates and grain are imported from Upper Egypt. Its inhabitants are Bejas. These people are black-skinned; they wrap themselves in yellow blankets and tie headbands about a finger-breadth wide round their heads. They do not give their daughters any share in their inheritance.'[16] The Reverend Samuel Lee translated this as 'Among the people the daughter never succeeds to property'[17] but both translations indicate that the Beja did not apply Islamic inheritance laws as they related to women.[18]

The Arab historian, Taqi al-Din Ahmad Al-Maqrizi (1364–1441), also referred to a matrilineal descent system among the Beja in his *Kitab* (1422): 'Their relationships follow the female line … they pass the inheritance to the daughter's son or sister's son, to the exclusion of the "son of the loins".'[19] Today the Bisharin still practise matrilocal marriage until the birth of the first child and inheritance passes from maternal uncle to nephew. Al-Maqrizi (1422) also noted that Arabian tribes, the Juheina (sent from Arabia by Caliph 'Umar in the seventh century) and the Rabi'a (the medieval invaders of Nubia) who settled on the west coast of the Red Sea, married daughters of local leaders and so secured the Beja chieftaincies through Beja traditions of matrilineal descent.[20]

As Suakin developed as a commercial centre, many merchants moved there from the Hijaz and several married local Beja women. As the Beja in the Suakin area traditionally inherited matrilineally, some of the Hijazis were able to use these inheritance rules to attain prominent tribal positions in the fourteenth century. When Ibn Battuta visited Suakin in 1328 (or 1332?) he found it was ruled by the Hijazi al-Sharif Zaid ibn Abi Numayy ibn 'Ajlan, son of the *amir* of Mecca. Sharif Zaid had inherited his position through his maternal uncles who were Beja.[21]

Many accounts of the region and its people by Classical geographers and

---

[16] *Ibn Battuta: Travels in Asia and Africa 1325–1354* on http://www.fordham.edu/halsall/source/1354–ibnbattuta.html

[17] Samuel Lee, *The Travels of Ibn Battuta* (London, Oriental Translation Committee, 1829). See also Yusf Fadl Hasan, *The Arabs and the Sudan from the Seventh to the Early Sixteenth Centuries* (Edinburgh, 1967), 73–9.

[18] This was challenged by G.W. Murray, *Sons of Ishmael* (London, George Routledge, 1935), 28, n.1: 'So the MS says, but the reverse would have been more correct'.

[19] Al-Maqrizi, *Khitab al-Mawaiz* (1422), I, 194, quoted in Murray (1935), 54.

[20] Murray, 303.

[21] Robert Berg, 'Suakin: Time and Tide', *Aramco World* 44/4 (August 1993) on http://www.saudiaramcoworld.com/issue/199304/default.htm

historians and by medieval Arab pilgrims were used as guides in the nineteenth and twentieth centuries by Burckhardt, Belzoni, Linant de Bellefonds, Sir J. G. Wilkinson and other travellers. J. L. Burckhardt, a superb Arabist, travelled in the region between 1812 and 1817 disguised as a poor merchant from India pretending to seek out a mythical cousin in Sennar.[22] He travelled miserably in 1813 with a caravan of slave traders from Daraw to Shendi via Abu Hamed, the same route that was taken by James Bruce in the 1770s. Burckhardt, who often used al-Maqrizi as a reference, also commented on reasons for matrilineal succession among the Beja: 'With them the son by the daughter, or son by the sister succeeds to property, to the exclusion of the true son, and they allege that the birth of the daughter's or sister's son is more certain, because at all events, whether it is the husband or someone else who is the father, he is always her son.'[23]

Burckhardt describes the ceremony of blessing the merchandise before the caravan departed: 'Ababda women appeared carrying earthenware vessels filled with burning coals which they placed before the loads and the couched camels. They threw salt on the embers and as the bluish flames rose the women cried: "May you be blessed in going and in coming!"'. After several days' journey through the desert, the caravan dismissed its camp followers including 'several dashing Egyptian dancing girls, the price of whose charms had increased in the mountains, in the same proportion as other commodities, and who had thus been able to acquire large sums of money in a very short time.'[24] These girls were deliberately abandoned by their guides when only a night's journey from the Nile and set upon by other 'Ababda who robbed them; stripped them naked and only then allowed them to proceed back to the Nile.

Burckhardt reached Shendi on April 17th 1814 after endless harassment from the Daraw slave traders who, thereafter, spent their evenings in brothels drinking *bouza*.[25] He recounts how goods including cow and camel meat, fresh and sour milk and chickpeas were brought into the market in Shendi by Beja girls to be bartered for millet (*dura*). Burckhardt's caravan from Shendi to Suakin was essentially trading in female slaves and they were in considerable fear of hostile attacks from fierce Bisharin, through whose territory they travelled.

Giovanni Belzoni also journeyed across the Eastern Desert between 1815 and 1819 and says incorrectly that the 'Ababda 'never intermarry with any of their own people', and, correctly , that an Ababda man also avoids his mother-

---

[22] J. L. Burckhardt, *Reisen in Nubian,* trans. from English (1820); *Travels in Nubia* (London, John Murray, 1919; 2nd edn; London, 1822).

[23] Burchhardt (1822), 458, quoted in A. Paul, *A History of the Beja Tribes of the Sudan* (London, Frank Cass, 1954), 64.

[24] Burckhardt (1822), 225.

[25] *Ibid.,* 240.

in-law.[26] According to G. W. Murray (1935), 'among the Beja a man still avoided his mother-in-law.'[27] It was certainly still the custom among the Amarar in the 1970s.

Linant de Bellefonds, searching for minerals in the Atbai in 1831 and 1832, also mentions the 'Ababda and the Bisharin.[28] He remarks on the beauty and easy virtue of Amarar and Balgab/Aliab women: 'l'on commerce avec la femme de son frère et les parents au même degré.' He noted that it was the women who made the matting for the tents in the country between the Nile and the Jabal Elba near the Red Sea: 'une troisième espèce de tentes que les indigènes confectionnent, en manière de cabanes, avec des branches d'arbres et des feuilles de doume ou palmier éventail tressées [*medemia argun*] et qu'ils tapissent intérieurement avec des étoffes grossières fabriquées par les femmes.'[29]

Whilst Lucie Duff Gordon was living in Luxor (see chapter 6 above) and on friendly terms with the 'Ababda shaykh there,[30] Karl Benjamin Klunzinger (1834–1914) was appointed by the Egyptian government as a sanitary and quarantine physician and lived in al-Qusayr from 1863 to1869 and again from 1876 to 1878. He produced a description of Upper Egypt that rivals Edward W. Lane's Cairene-based *Manners and Customs of Modern Egyptians* in terms of its quality and delight. Klunzinger was able to draw upon his experiences and confidences he gained as a doctor to describe the ways of life of local women in detail.[31]

He begins his book with the description of women in the image of ghosts, inert and insubstantial: 'Round the walls of the house before us a ghost-like being steals, the whole figure from the crown of the head to the feet – which are alone visible – carefully enveloped in a wide mantle, which falls in numerous folds; we are told that it is one of the fair sex.' But he goes on to give a fairer picture of women in the Eastern Desert. He not only described 'an invisible female voice issuing from a house' but also emotions of curiosity and contact. Klunzinger reports on a wide range of social and physical environments, fascinated as much by sea life and coral, as by superstition and domestic livelihoods. He goes beyond the line taken by Jean-Louis Ampère who declared that 'the Orient is for me, today, like a masked women who has revealed only

---

[26] G. Belzoni, *Narrative of the Operations and Recent Discoveries [...] in Egypt and Nubia* (London, 1821), 304–13.

[27] Murray, 55.

[28] Linant de Bellefonds Bey, *L'Étbaye. Pays habité par les Arabes bicharieh. Géographie, ethnologie, mines d'or* (Paris s.d. 1884), (notes date to the years 1832–1833), 188.

[29] *Ibid.*, 134.

[30] Lucie Duff Gordon, *Letters from Egypt, 1863–1865* (London, Macmillan, 1865).

[31] C. B. Klunzinger, *Upper Egypt: its people and products* (London, Blackie, 1878) 51–52.

her face' and describes the exoticism of women's veils in the streets of Qusayr:[32]

> a creature entirely enveloped in a large brown or striped grey cloth [...] another
> creature [...] squeezes itself close to a wall till we have passed by, drawing the
> cloth firmly over its face. [...] Wishing to behave with propriety we behave as
> if we had seen nothing [...] after a few minutes both of us [...] seized with
> curiosity, turn around at the same moment.[33]

Klunzinger's reality is remote from a modern feminist perspective: it is curiosity
rather than seduction that is on their minds.

Klunzinger describes the dress of 'Ababda women: 'The women clothe
themselves with white cloth drawn under one or both armpits so that one or
both shoulders and arms remain free, and over this a large outer wrapper, also
generally white, which can conceal the whole form; in winter instead of a
wrapper, a mantle of brown woollen stuff is also worn similar to those worn by
female peasants of Nile valley.' The 'women plait hair their from the crown
down into many rows of plaits, the foremost of which, in front of the ear, has
more freedom of movement than the others.' He also added that 'like all other
women they believe that they are not attractive.'[34]

Unlike most nineteenth-century travel writers, Klunzinger concentrated his
descriptions on married women. Marriage vows were rarely violated: lovers
would meet in lonely mountain gorges but as all the 'Ababda were good trackers,
this was very risky, though Klunzinger found that 'on the caravan route and
outskirts of larger villages there are even a few Abadeh prostitutes.'[35] Klunzinger
includes a section on the 'Entertainments of Women',[36] of their *fantas'eh* in the
weeks before a circumcision or marriage. 'They meet together every day (seldom
at night) in the house where the entertainments are given, where they sing, beat
the darabuka or hand-drum and the tambourine. Men must not be spectators,
not even the master of the house. The professional singers (*almeh*), more virtuous
than the dancing-girls, generally exhibit their powers only in the harem, and the
men listen to their charming songs through the latticed windows of the women's
apartments.' Like Belzoni, Klunzinger noted the strange Beja custom of a
husband avoiding his mother-in-law. 'When a woman has been married she
must never see her own mother afterwards. The young husband always removes
far away from the parental family of his bride, chiefly in order *to avoid his mother-
in-law.*' He considered polygamy was expensive and only practised by shaykhs.
Klunzinger's perceptions are based on in-depth understanding of his neighbours,

---

[32] Jean-Jacques Ampière as quoted by Harper in 'Recovering the Other', *Critical
Matrix* 1: 3 (1985), 2.

[33] Klunzinger, 40–2.

[34] *Ibid.*, 252.

[35] *Ibid.*, 265–6.

[36] *Ibid.*, 193.

written after many years' experience and immersion in the local culture, albeit speaking as a man, for what other perspective could he provide?

Conclusion

The women of the Eastern Desert were little affected by the economic and social changes to the way of life for women in the Nile Valley between 1800 and 1950, a way of life that has been carefully described by Tucker and others. The women of the Eastern Desert were beyond the cotton plantations, away from mass migrations to the cities. Life, for them, continued largely unchanged, as it does in eastern Sudan today, for the state was unable or unwilling to regulate economic and social life in the area at the margins of Egyptian society. For European women visiting the region their own experiences of the Eastern Desert were essentially transient. For them, the desert was a place of entertainment or a transit route to the pleasures of India or the Nile Valley.

The 'Orient' is not just a geographical region but a concept which has become politically and geographically charged. In a succession of sympathetic and empathetic descriptions, the women of the Eastern Desert have escaped many of the myths associated with Orientalism. Timothy Mitchell claims, in *Colonizing Egypt*, that 'what is outside is paradoxically what makes the West what it is, the excluded yet integral part of its identity and power.'[37] If the Eastern Desert is also outside the normal parameters of Orientalism with all its colonial associations, where does this leave our perceptions of the women of the Eastern desert? As Andrea B. Rugh states, 'despite their extensive travels, trading fish to Qina and camels to Daraw […] the Beja remain, as far as Egypt is concerned, a backwater of unique dress styles.'[38] Curiously, in their dress they look eastwards, for today the women wear bright-coloured red, blue, green and yellow saris and nose-rings inspired by Indian traditions via caravan and sea trade routes. It is not only their dress style that appears to be in a backwater: Beja women have been consistently excluded from the Orientalism debate. If women are the 'other' in Oriental society and 'Ababda marginalised in Upper Egypt, women of the Eastern Desert can only be an enigmatic 'marginalised other'. Or is there, indeed, a cacophony of notions and images of the 'other' that are far more complex than any Orientalist approach to women in the Eastern Desert?

---

[37] Mitchell, 166.
[38] Andrea B. Rugh, *Reveal and Conceal: dress in contemporary Egypt* (Cairo, AUC, 1986).

Bibliography

Belzoni, G., *Narrative of the Operations and Recent Discoveries* [...] *in Egypt and Nubia* (London, 1821).

Broadhurst, R. J. C., *The Travels of Ibn Jubayr* (London, Jonathan Cape, 1952).

Burckhardt, J.-L*., Travels in Nubia* (London, John Murray, 1819; 2nd edn; London, 1822).

Buxton, Edward North. ed., *On Either Side of the Red Sea. With illustrations of the granite ranges of the Eastern Desert of Egypt, and of Sinai.* By H. M. B., C. E. B. and T. B. (London, Edward Stanford, 1895).

Daly, Martin, ed., *Cambridge History of Egypt* (Cambridge, Cambridge University Press, 1998).

Ross E. Dunn, *The Adventures of Ibn Battuta* (Berkeley, Ca., University of California Press, 1986).

Edwards, Amelia, *One Thousand Miles up the Nile* (London, Longman, 1877).

Elwood, Mrs. Catherine [Anne Katherine], *Narrative of a Journey Overland by the Continent of Europe, Egypt and the Red Sea to India, including a Residence there and a voyage home, 1825–1828* (London, H. Colburn and R. Bentley, 1830).

Gordon, Lucie Duff*, Letters from Egypt, 1863–1865* (London, Macmillan, 1865).

Hasan, Yusf Fadl, *The Arabs and the Sudan from the Seventh to the Early Sixteenth Centuries* (Edinburgh, 1967).

Linant de Bellefonds Bey*, L'Étbaye. Pays habité par les Arabes bicharieh. Géographie, ethnologie, mines d'or* (Paris s. d. 1884). (The notes date to the years 1832–1833).

Klunzinger, C. B., *Upper Egypt: its people and products* (London, Blackie, 1878).

Mabro, Judith, *Veiled Half-Truths* (London, I.B. Tauris, 1991).

Martineau, H., *Eastern Life*, 3 vols (London, 1848).

Melman, Billie, *Women's Orients: English women and the Middle East 1718–1918* (Ann Arbor, The University of Michigan Press, 1992).

Mitchell, Timothy, *Colonising Egypt* (Cambridge, Cambridge University Press, 1988; Berkeley, University of California Press, 1991).

Murray, G. W., *Sons of Ishmael* (London, George Routledge, 1935).

Nieuwkerk, Karin van., *"A Trade like any Other": female singers and dancers in Egypt* (Austin, University of Texas Press, 1995).

Paul, A. *A History of the Beja Tribes of the Sudan* (Cambridge, Cambridge University Press, 1954; repr. London, Frank Cass, 1971).

Rugh, Andrea B., *Reveal and Conceal: dress in contemporary Egypt* (Cairo, AUC, 1986).

Said, Edward W., *Orientalism* (London, Routledge and Kegan Paul, 1978).

Starkey, Janet and Okasha El Daly (ed.), *Desert Travellers from Herodotus to T.E. Lawrence* (Durham, ASTENE, 2000).

Tucker, Judith E., *Women in Nineteenth-Century Egypt* (Cambridge, Cambridge University Press, 1985).

Wilkinson, J. G., *Handbook for Travellers in Egypt* (London, John Murray, 1847).

Yeğenoğlu, Meyda, *Colonial Fantasies: towards a feminist reading of Orientalism* (Cambridge, Cambridge University Press, 1998).

11. Archaeologists' Wives as Travel Writers

Elizabeth French

When in the winter of 2002 the exhibition 'Agatha Christie and Archaeology' was held in the British Museum, accompanied by the reissue of her auto-biography, *Come, Tell Me How You Live*, and her novel, *Murder in Mesopotamia*, set on an excavation in Iraq, three other books by archaeologists' wives came to mind. But these were by women who were not already distinguished authors in their own right.

The three women all worked in the Near East in the years following World War II and their books were written between 1949 and 1959. The accounts evoke landscapes and lifestyles which have changed almost beyond recognition during the last half century and the record they give is thus as important as any from previous centuries, for the archaeologist's wife has access to information and other advantages which are not available to other visitors.

Unlike other travellers, the archaeologist and his team remain for several months in one place and may come back repeatedly over the years. The books thus give a long-term account of a small area, rather that a short-term account of a wider area. In this the archaeologist works more as an anthropologist and many have written important anthropological studies in addition to excavation reports. Other differences lie in the access they may have to the local culture through good (or ever improving) knowledge of the language and the presence of a long-suffering government representative who can be asked for endless explanations as well as entertaining any children who may be present.

When Margaret Wheeler, an Australian and Sir Mortimer's third wife, published *Walls of Jericho* in 1956, the publishers Chatto and Windus were 'cashing in' on the interest occasioned by the discoveries of 'the dawn of civilization' and the amazing early art – of around the seventh millennium BC – that accompanied it. This is clear from the reissue of the book two years later by the Readers Union, an edition which again included the sketches by the author and some excellent photographs. Escape and recovery from wartime hardship and austerity

Kim (Margaret) Wheeler with the Jericho staff visiting Qumran, 1954 or 1955. Photograph by Linda A. Witherill of the Jericho staff. Standing, left to right: Kim Wheeler, Kay Kenyon, Père de Vaux, Charles Burney, Oliver Unwin. Behind: John Carswell, Ann Battershill. Seated: Dorothy Marshall.

were mental as well as physical. In the surprisingly well-expressed foreword, that laconic lady Kathleen Kenyon, the leader of the expedition, speaks of 'the way of things on a dig', of 'distilling history from the reluctant elements left by the crumbling ruins of town and cemetery.' Quite rightly she describes the book as an accurate but popular prelude to the official reports. She certainly realised that it relieved her of one publication that might otherwise have been expected of her.

Margaret Wheeler weaves an intricate narrative through time in two dimensions. As a traveller she describes her journey to the site, at that time a lengthy one in a *servis* (shared) taxi from Beirut via Damascus and Amman, where the problems of no common language are mitigated by the sharing of cigarettes (was there an equivalent for the nineteenth century traveller?). She continues with the events of the season and on to the inevitable packing up. But into this she also describes, in chronological order through more than eight millennia, the formation and history of the site by the perpetual spring and its various inhabitants. She even gives excellent summary introductions to such then new-fangled techniques as Carbon-14 dating and the beginnings of environmental archaeology.

The excavation was based around a water mill, a sturdy Ottoman building of a century or so earlier, at the base of the Jericho Tell. Excavation was carried out not only on the Tell, a uniquely early site where mudbrick architecture, so important in the formation of such tells (*hüyüks*, *magoulas* or whatever), was enclosed by a series of formidable stone walls, but also in the many tombs which were continually being discovered as the authorities dug trenches for latrines in the Palestinian refugee village to the north of the site. From a socio-political standpoint, one of the most important features of this book is the account it gives of the refugee village at this time. With a sense of justice that could well be emulated, the original villagers of Jericho were employed as workmen on the tell, while the refugees dug the tombs lying beneath their own mudbrick settlement.

The next account also deals with a mixed group of workmen but this time it is the Arabs and Kurds of north-east Iraq. Linda Braidwood – who like her husband lived to well over ninety and died only in January 2003 (after in fact I had begun work on this paper) – in her book *Digging Beyond the Tigris* published in 1959 by Simon and Schuster, tells of the work of the Chicago's Oriental Institute at Jarmo (in the Zagros foothills of north-eastern Iraq) and adjacent earlier sites. Margaret Wheeler had mentioned Jarmo in passing as a site almost contemporary with Jericho but without Jericho's impressive walls.

The site was excavated in 1950–51. Unlike Jericho it was so remote that a road had to be built for the expedition vehicles to get there. The archaeologists started from scratch with the order of 50,000 mud bricks for the construction of a dig house – under the supervision of their Egyptian foreman – and we can follow in considerable detail everything necessary in the organisation of an expedition. This would have served admirably as a text book for the practical archaeology course at the Institute of Archaeology in London at that time and is considerably more lively than the fascinating but unadorned lists of equipment in many excavators' notebooks.

For the archaeologist particular interest lies in comparing not only the actual excavation methods but also the two sponsoring institutions, the renowned and, even by then, venerable Oriental Institute of the University of Chicago and the London University Institute of Archaeology, which was of such importance to the development of post-war archaeology in the United Kingdom and its scientific offshoots. It is amusing too to compare another account of infant Carbon-14 work. For many archaeologists the account is particularly nostalgic amid the recent history of Iraq in recalling a period of exploration there, a generation later than that described by Agatha Christie but still with a background not only of the excellent Department of Antiquities, built in part on the work of Gertrude Bell, and also of provisions traditionally bought at the ubiquitous grocery company Spinneys and equipment borrowed from the then Iraq Petroleum Company.

The text for all its detail is not as didactic as Margaret Wheeler's and the style

Linda Braidwood with the Jarmo team, 1951. Reproduced courtesy of the Oriental Institute of the University of Chicago; Digging Beyond the Tigris, *Fig. 15. Standing, left to right: Sabri Shukry, Bruce Howe, Dr Naji al-Asil, Robert J. Braidwood, Fredrik Barth, Robert McC. Adams. Seated, left to right: Elizabeth West (Fitzhugh), Linda Braidwood, Vivian Browman (Morales).*

is more relaxed. The events of the season, however, are similar with highlights of fantasias and weddings where the women of foreign groups like these are allowed to see the customs of both men and women even in a Muslim country. With the expedition's focus on the origins of agriculture in the 'Fertile Crescent' it is perhaps not surprising that Linda Braidwood gives more information on animals, birds and plants. Also they were on site for a full nine months and had a better chance of seeing seasonal variations. They were also much further from base and American expeditions – particularly such long-lasting ones – seem to require more 'home touches' than others. Even so, much time and energy had to be expended locally on shopping. Any expedition is lucky that has been able to hire a competent cook who will shop for anything (and usually find it) as was the case at Jarmo.

Mary Gough had never been to Turkey when she went in the spring of 1949, alone with her husband Michael, to survey in Cilicia. As she tells us at the start of her book, titled *The Plain and the Rough Places* (Chatto and Windus, 1955) after

Mary Gough on a horse. Photograph by Dr U. Bahadir Alkim. The Plain and the Rough Places, *cover and fig.8.*

the description of the area by the Greek geographer Strabo, 'I am not an archaeologist myself and so I deal mainly with the sort of life that we led and the people that we met.' In fact Mary Gough was originally a naval architect and her mapping and drawing skills were of great importance to their work. Indeed she later drew the map for her husband's important publication, *The Classical Map of Asia Minor.* From the first pages she plunges the reader into the contrasts of Anatolia: delays because of snow or mud, the heat, the bustle of the market, shopping in a provincial centre, bargaining for transport but above all the distances and the landscape.

In this, her account is similar to those of the other authors but we have moved not only westward to Turkey but onward through time. The Goughs were concentrating on what Linda Braidwood refers to as 'the historic time range' – in fact recording of largely Graeco-Roman and Byzantine standing monuments – though the term 'standing' is perhaps misleading. Turkey is probably unique in having such a large number of large sites with major stone-built monuments not overbuilt in later times but merely overgrown by heavy *garique*-type vegetation. Indeed one such site, Termessus, in the hills above Antalya, has been left in this state as a National Park and tourist attraction with merely a few paths cut through the shrubs. Elsewhere, as Mary Gough says, the monuments have suffered from 'battle, wind, rain, earthquake and mankind'.

She tells us that comfortably seated at home they had listed the sites on which they intended to work, as it happened in alphabetical order; thus it was that they started out at Anarvarza in the hills above the Cilician plain and worked their way both through the alphabet and westward each season to Cilicia Aspera.

There were other aspects in which this expedition differed from the first two. The account covers not just one season but all nine though they are blended together in the narrative. Thus we see not only the benefits of the Goughs' growing fluency in Turkish, but the improvements to the life style of the inhabitants: better roads and transport, development in local government, the widening outlook that access to radios gave the population.

It is not only the monuments in Turkey that suffer from the inquisitiveness of the local inhabitants and the Goughs were more subject to this than the members of a larger team would have been. Only in the later years did others join them. But with growing communication skills and the growth of habits of self-protection their initial unease in the face of this unwanted attention was conquered as we are told in a chapter of candid honesty.

Mary Gough was well versed in the accounts of all those who had travelled before in the area, from St Paul, tentmaker of Tarsus, and the unfortunate Barbarosa to Colonel Leake riding through the pass from Karaman arrayed in Tartar dress. She also had a good eye for the bizarre and absurd and a telling turn of phrase. Both Goughs were deservedly prized dinner guests to enliven the Embassy circuit in Ankara later: they were both brilliant raconteurs and Michael Gough was a formidable mimic.

The simple enjoyment of reading these books, even rereading them critically for an assessment such as this, is considerable but it is difficult to rationalise. It comes partly indeed from nostalgia but also from the myriad of intriguing details of which they tell us. It is perhaps less clear why they were written, especially by people as busy as these authors. The need to fill long winter evenings is not frequent among archaeologists' wives. Moreover it was almost certainly not 'for the record' but as an offshoot of the work itself. Here we can see a contrast between these authors and more recent scholars. Recently in the preface to an excellent general book on an important and very interesting project, the leader of the expedition felt it necessary to say, 'fieldwork is not a holiday' and to list the tribulations of their existence in the field. Such a team is now large and the pressure of work heavy throughout – the *joi de vivre* seems to have gone. Kay Kenyon sums up this component for us when she says: 'the morale of the party is enormously sustained by the interest of our surroundings.' All of these authors belonged to a generation who wrote long descriptive letters home, who had already transferred their reactions to words. There may be some intention of passing on the story to the next generation. There may too have been some idea of telling it once in print instead of repeatedly to those who ask so kindly, 'Did you have a good holiday?' when one returns from an arduous season of field work. When Agatha Christie titled her autobiography *Come, Tell Me How You Live*, written as it was during the difficult days of World War II, she seems to have had this in mind but as well we find a deep emotion in her closing words – ones which all these authors might well have written – '*Inshallah*, I shall go there again, and the things that I love shall not have perished from this earth.'

Index